THE

DONNER

PARTY

George Keithley

GEORGE BRAZILLER

NEW YORK

Portions of *The Donner Party* have previously ap-
peared in the following publications, to whose editors
grateful acknowledgment is made: *Harper's*, *The
Massachusettes Review*, and *The North American Review*.

Standard Book Number: 0–8076–1235–9
Library of Congress Catalog Card Number: 75–183185
Printed in the United States of America
First paperback printing, October 1989

For my father and mother

CONTENTS

Book One

Book Two

Book Three

Book One

1

Taking the Trail

I am George Donner a dirt farmer
who left the snowy fields
around Springfield, Illinois
in the fullness of my life

and abandoned the land
where we had been successful
and prosperous people

and brought a party of eighty men
women and children
west by wagon.

For weeks my wife
Tamsen was the talk of women
meeting in the marketplace

keeping warm indoors
pricing yards of dry goods
and rolls of ribbon

while we laid up large stores
for our journey
across the unsettled country.

But the last pools of ice
had disappeared from the road
when we set out.

This was during the damp days
of early April when the trees shake
off their snow

in the orchard and wood
and begin to bud.
That winter we had read

reports printed in the States
on California climate where the soil
is sewn with streams in every season.

All year you can smell the bloom in the air
and farm the fertile land
lying in the yellow valley heat.

And so we prepared to go
and packed our pewter and plates.
Carefully we chose our daughters' clothes.

Their winter coats and woolen leggings
were laid in a trunk which we lifted
by two ebony handles.

Tamsen sorted out the silks
and bolts of bright cloth,
cambric and calico

and much more plain muslin.
When the wagons were drawn onto the lawn and loaded
I assured her,

"Once we're there
it will seem worth all
the work and time it took."

Then like an afterthought
a teamster brought out Tamsen's tallow
and a long rifle box crammed with her candles.

He wheeled the wagons wide of the house
and around a chopping block buried in the shade
of the smoke shed, and I rode alongside

as the oxen swelled ahead in the harness.
My family led the line of nine wagons at the start.
Six were filled with freight.

In mine were salt and spice
and bushels of meal,
dry fruit and rice;

my wife wanted to hold
our infant daughter
Frances on her lap;

Eliza, six years old,
and Georgia, four,
were seated on the floor.

My brother Jacob joined us
with his wife Elizabeth
and their three boys.

And our friends the family
of James Reed, who made money
in mines and rails and carpentry

and drove a huge house wagon
equipped with passenger door
and collapsible stairs

a portable stove
and a rug on the floor
and a table and chairs;

the permanent seats
were screwed onto springs
to provide a relaxing ride.

With Reed in the rear
we followed the fat flanks of our cattle
across familiar fields

until the green skin
of the Sangamon river could be seen
sunning itself like a lazy snake.

Flies the size of bees
buzz and flit
about the bank

where we built our fire
for supper and began
to pitch our tents in the grass

and gather our belongings.
When Tamsen found
her looking-glass

she shook the shawl
off her shoulders,
and her green eyes

appeared to glow
in the hot shadow
of her auburn hair.

While we sat there
by the flames our friends
from miles around rode up.

We sang and danced
and little Eliza
and Georgia jumped with delight

though Frances fell asleep
in my arms before
we cried, "Goodbye!"

to our guests
and they withdrew
in the night calling,

"God be with you!"
and turned home
toward the dark farms.

When they were gone
my wife and I
by lantern light

took the time
to rearrange items
that the first day's drive had jarred loose.

It didn't damage anything of use to us.
That night on our knees
we looked at all our luxuries . . .

The hand mirrors and
bead sacks and calf-bound cookbooks.
A botanical collection kept in a box.

"We own too many mirrors,"
I said and she agreed. Finally
we sipped our brandy and then we slept.

A rainstorm rattled the birch trees.
The bark gleamed like white paint at sunrise
when a driver rode out to scout the river.

The next day he trotted back and reported,
"The Mississippi looks awful.
It's at the flood stage still.

Crowds come up with their cattle
and camp on top of the hills
waiting for the water to settle."

The wagons sagged with moisture
while we sat
in the dripping light.

Then it grew quiet.
A pet cat crept out.
A horse pissed in the pasture.

We started off
toward the riverbed.
On the border of a black field

where the rain of recent days
had drained down
in the furrows

our party saw
a Mormon farm
fly up in a blaze.

A victim of this disaster
stood in the mud of the road.
His family flocked around

while the fire consumed
the roof and frame.
The barn and a cluster

of side coops
slowly collapsed;
the tongues of flame

ate up the poultry
and livestock left in a pen
as we rode by.

When we arrived
the river ran high with rain and thaw
but the ferry was able

to float us over
and it could carry our cattle as well.
On the west bank we put the oxen under yoke

and we fell in line once more.
We drove for many miles
across Missouri and saw

slash marks on the hills
where settlers already
had cleared the land

stripping away the wood.
This rapid cutting allowed
the rain to erode the slopes

so the streams overflowed—
our horses chopped the soft sod
and where the trail grew narrow

we heard the tired trek
of the cattle at our back
shik-plok, shik-plok, in the muck.

We approached Independence
under a blanket of brown sky.
2,000 tents stood outside of town.

On the east bank
of the Missouri river we found
teamsters and drivers wanting work

and trappers and dogs and runaways
and travellers of every kind
keeping an eye on the water.

I walked onto the mudflats
by the busy river where
the ground bubbled around my boots.

I returned to town before dark.
In a dry goods store I spoke
with Charles Stanton, a native of New York.

He was a small man with large eyes
such as our livestock have . . .
animals who only need to find

the grass which the land supplies
everywhere under their gaze.
A few words told his story.

"To make money I moved
to Chicago," he said.
"But I went bankrupt in a hurry.

I won't sit idle where I know
that I can't earn
a living any longer."

I encouraged him
to keep us company.
As we met other emigrants our party grew.

Mrs Murphy was a widow
with four boys. Their sister
Sarah had married William Foster

a man less than half as old
as I am but as bald
as anyone I've ever seen—

on the whole crown
of his head he had
no more hair than a stone.

We met poor Patrick Breen
who sailed from Ireland a year ago
with his wife and six boys and a baby girl.

A large man named McCutchen
brought his bride who was big with child
and due any day.

Jacob had taken a teamster named Noah James.
I was in need of a man myself when I heard
of a half-breed called Jean Ba'tiste

who swore he had been west before.
"I remember the whole route.
I learned it by heart."

I hired him on.
Then the water dropped
and the delay was over.

Morning, the 12th of May,
riding over the river,
we left the States under oily skies.

500 wagons travelled together
and in no particular order
thru miles of yellow meadow

where slim stems of goldenrod
glistened after the rain.
At dusk we drew up to a stream.

Reed cast from the bank and caught
catfish with whiskers like wire.
So we shovelled a fire

into several shallow holes
and fried the fish
on the red coals.

One young father,
Bill Eddy, set his traps
for small game.

I searched my satchel
for our reading matter
and at supper there was talk

of Lansford Hastings' book
The Emigrants' Guide
and Frémont's *Report, with Maps* . . .

A smaller party picked a hill
to camp on and came down
by the stream to meet us.

They were Germans who still
spoke their native tongue
as well as our own.

One gentleman by the name
of Keseberg and his wife
introduced the others.

Among these were
Wolfinger and his wife
and an old man named Hardkoop.

The men were armed
for safe travel
with a knife or pistol

and some wore riding suits
displaying scrolls of golden thread.
The ladies wore lace and immaculate linen.

They were polite people
and we urged them to join our party.
Then Tamsen put

lumps of bread
and beef and peas
in one big tin pot.

Margaret Reed
baked raisin biscuits
while her children took over

trying to nurse
their grandmother
who fell ill with a fever.

That night her family knelt
on the floor to pray
for her soul.

She died before dawn
and a box had to be built.
The morning sun was steaming hot

and the wind leaped like a flame
around our feet while
we dug into the dirt

preparing a plot
above the Big Blue river.
At noon we carried her coffin out.

A part-time preacher
holding his book
watched us work.

Reed's teamster
Milt Elliot
and a gunsmith named Denton

cut her tombstone
and hammered it into the hill
and we returned

toward the wall
of wagons
wedged into a circle

where Jacob's horse
and mine were picketed
with Reed's prize mare.

There in the shade
of an old oak we stopped
to wipe the spades.

They came clean enough
but the ground gave off
an unforgettable odor

which remained in the air
long afterward and we
could smell the black loam
even while we walked back.

2
I Am the Judge

The Big Blue river was a yellow brown color
when we rolled our wagons onto a raft
and coaxed the cattle into the water.
Slowly they made their way across.

Sunlight slid from their flanks
as the cows climbed out of the current
and waded wide-eyed up the shore

wandering into a field
where the grass stinks
from a profusion of wild onions.

One source said the Sioux
had killed many Crows near here
though we saw nothing

but the black earth
of an abandoned campsite.
At night I strolled past the fire

where Keseberg and two young men,
Reinhardt and Spitzer,
were joking in German.

Keseberg kept a buffalo robe
folded over his knees.
I asked him, "Whose is it?"

"What's mine,"
he replied,
"is no affair of yours."

I wouldn't let go.
I needed to know where he found it.
So he explained,

"Yesterday morning
we saw some trash
back there near the river."

Ba'tiste came over.
"I suppose
someone should tell you

they pulled these things
off the funeral perch
of a dead Sioux.

Some of us
saw them do it.
They took a watch

and other pieces—
whatever they could reach
standing up in the stirrup."

I didn't believe it.
But both men heard him
and drifted away from the fire.

I ran to tell Reed.
"They robbed a scaffold.
They stole the robe

that covered the corpse.
And the body is still out.
The Sioux will come back to it."

Others were worried besides ourselves.
Denton demanded the lives of the thieves.
"Take them to a tree and hang them both."

"Custom," I said, "requires
that we banish
the person responsible."

Reed said it was insane
to provide these people
the protection of the law.

"When the Sioux learn
what was done
we'll be dead men."

While this quarrel
continued we
were losing time.

Reed asked me,
"George,
what do you suggest?"

"We'll search the men,"
I said. "Return
every item

to its place
so the body will appear
to be untouched.

Then we'll ride
back to camp and bring
this business before a court.

If all goes well
Keseberg can stand trial
tomorrow night."

My plan met with approval.
I ran to our tent
and told Tamsen,

"Find some way to conceal
everything of value . . .
Nothing will be safe."

When Reed arrived we hurried off.
Keseberg rode between our two mares
as we travelled quietly under the stars.

We watched them dissolve in the dawn
and the sun rose early to reveal
a grey haze that hung upon the grass.

Later it lifted so we saw
a strange glow in the distance
like little patches of snow

which proved to be the burial ground
where white skulls were arranged in rings
at four corners on the prairie.

The corpse lay
in the midst of these
on a scaffold of painted poles.

A brood of buzzards glided over
the poles supporting
the dead body

left there by the living
to dry in the open air.
We folded his robe over him.

Keseberg laid the watch beside his head.
Then we turned back riding hard
and reached camp after dark;

we dismounted among
two dozen men
whose movements made

an uncertain glimmer,
the gunbarrels more orange than blue
in the torchlight.

Jacob declared nominations
now in order.
They closed quickly.

By voice vote
I was chosen
to be the judge.

I didn't wish it
but it was only right.
By age and authority the job fell to me.

I took my seat on the crate
my brother brought out
and he stayed put.

My friend James Reed, familiar
with procedure, a Master Mason,
presented the case against the German.

"To protect one another
and guarantee
general safety

we live by the laws
of the United States.
We do this willingly

with the common
consent of the people.
Nobody wants trouble.

We remember our rights
and keep the peace
when we're able.

Nevertheless to plunder
the dead as you did
is reprehensible!

It places every
family in jeopardy
of a raid

in retaliation
which may mean rape and murder.
A man who will endanger

every other member
deserves no mercy."
Here he was interrupted.

Leaving his friends,
Keseberg came forward.
He said, "Sit down

you stinking saint
with this pair of pigs
that you call your court

so you can enjoy
the large esteem
that they lavish on you.

You might even learn
your neighbors' love
has a legal limit

and won't allow
an unjust judgment
on a man who is innocent.

What crime did I commit?
Does it have any name?
If a man steals

from a building
that's burglary
and if he steals

from a person
it may be robbery
but if he takes property

which belongs to a corpse
and keeps it for a time
and brings it back again

he does no more harm
than many men who farm
the land or sell real estate.

Why am I on trial tonight?
I took what I could use,
it wasn't yours.

But I will say this:
if I did endanger
the life of anyone

the harm has been undone.
We're back where we began.
As for the need to atone

or make amends
for my mistake
my conscience is my own concern.

And one other point
which I wish to mention . . .
You can claim no legitimate jurisdiction.

No law applies to this territory.
You people have no authority
to hold this trial."

So saying, he stood
awaiting an answer
while he looked the other way

keeping his eyes on the crowd
not wanting to watch me
deliver my decision.

"It's by convention
established in previous parties
that we can convene a court

consider a case
and prescribe the penalty.
A precedent of that sort is enough.

I believe every person pities his wife,
who must suffer his absence
when it's not her fault,

but we'll banish him
without his weapons or any meat
to learn a decent sense of guilt."

I kicked the crate aside.
When I walked away
Reinhardt caught my coat.

"Are you so damned holy
you can tell a man to stay
or send him out in the dark to die?"

"Please," I said, "try to realize
that this is necessary
for our protection."

I collected Keseberg's guns
and locked them both in a box.
McCutchen kept him under guard.

He was jerked on his horse
when his hands had been bound.
He was led from the light by a guide

who walked him thru a thicket
to the edge of the prairie
where he was untied.

When I returned to the tent
Tamsen took my hand.
With her help I felt

where her careful stitch
left an inconspicuous patch
over a bulge in the bedding.

"While you were gone I sewed
our money in the quilt
for safe keeping."

We were too worried
that night to sleep.
We sat up feeding a fire,

hearing a choir of crickets
chirring away in the grass
until morning made it clear

that we were out of danger
and we left for Ash Hollow,
a water hole below Scotts Bluff
where we could camp awhile, to our relief.

3

The Platte River and the Prairie

Buffalo bathed in the brown river
widening the water
while the other half
of the herd was feeding in a field.

It was a warm June morning,
even the boys on sentry duty
sat down on the bank

watching the dung-colored cows
wallow in the water
that flooded around their flanks

so we weren't prepared
when the young Pawnee
came into camp . . .

Some wore paint smeared
down their cheeks
and they were careful

to shave
the whole head except a scalp-lock,
a single shock of hair on top of the skull

to which they tied
a thatch of hair taken from the tail
of a deer and dyed blood-red.

Every brave
had brought his rifle
and wanted to prove his skill

so we went out to a tall patch
of prairie grass to see them shoot
(you could hardly call it a hunt at all)

and they knelt down as one by one
each man put on a wolf skin,
a complete pelt

from head to tail
long enough to cover
his body when he bent over.

Almost at once
the indian acquired
a queer kind of innocence

as though he had lost
the gift of reason
and in its absence

he looked a little
less stiff than
the rest of us,

seeming to move
more like an animal
that must follow its feelings.

His lower legs still showed
and his hairless
human hands hung out.

The head of the wolf hid the bald
skull of the man inside.
Under its jaws his eyes glowed.

This was a disguise he wore
to make the buffalo
ignore him as if

he was a wolf
who came around to clean
the carcass of a dead cow . . .

They filled their rifles now
and fell on all fours and crawled
away like wolves in the waving grass.

While the sun beat down on us
the buffalo bent eating the green wind
in which their faces disappeared.

The hunters on their hands and knees
approached the herd and not one was seen.
When they shot a big cow our children cheered!

They killed nine or ten more.
Some people prefer
the tender tongue.

We cut whatever part
we felt we could cook—
the hump behind the skull

and the huge hump ribs
and the side ribs too,
we wanted to try it all.

With men like McCutchen,
the gunsmith Denton,
and Bill Eddy and Reed

I sat down to drink
the animal's bile
out of a bowl.

But the meat I ate
was much too rich
to settle in my belly.

When it came to me
I shut my mouth,
leaped to my feet

and raced over
to the low trees by the river
and retched in the grass where no one could see.

I swallowed some whisky and I felt all right.
We kept our camp another night
but nobody bothered curing meat.

We had enough beef for everyone.
It was the one item
we were able to buy at a bargain.

(In the States, in the river towns,
butcher's meat sold cheap in the streets.
The finest rounds for 2¢ a pound.)

*

We were lounging in our camp
late on a Sunday evening
when we received word

of a marriage performed
in the train travelling
ahead of our own.

A man named Moultry
had married Mary Lard
in a simple ceremony

after which a cake
complete with candles
was set before the guests.

Then one morning we left the river
far behind us and a small bird flew
round and round, flirting in the field.

We loafed out in a lazy line and heard
the meadowlark's song
tsee-oo, tsee-air, all day long.

We followed the fire
of the summer sun
across shrivelled creeks

and past wrinkled ponds
of rainwater revolving on the prairie,
and made poor time as the country grew hilly.

Late one day we stopped
where a grove of ash trees gripped the wall
of the sunken slough called Ash Hollow.

Parties passing this way
ahead of us had watered at the place
and left it looking like a swamp.

The marsh was marked by cattle tracks.
Spears of grass were trampled in the mud.
The trail to the water was as slick as grease.

We backed down, sliding our wagons down
the slope a few feet at a time.
Drivers had to drag the cattle.

I waited while
our stock started to drink
and then I walked off with my wife.

Hand in hand we went
up the slope to lie
beneath the trees.

The sun no longer burned
the sky, and we had seen
the hills grow more severe.

But it was still gentle
green country like the kind
we came from,

a patchwork prairie
broken by woods and farms
where we made our homes,

and more than happy
to find ourselves alone
at last we turned
into each other's arms.

4
Ash Hollow

Your green eyes
seeing the hollow
sinking in the shade
grow dim—

Time let me
lay with you a long
time let me

play with your hair
around my hand
your warm

tongue lag, linger
or slide slow
time let me

go and race
a fair race my
legs against yours

ash leaves vanish
off the cool rise
the sky

and the wide hills
draw down night
on this high place
and your green eyes.

5
Keseberg Comes Back

One morning in the last week of June
we left the muddy lip of the marsh,
all the wagons in one column
of many-colored canvas

brown or white
or blue bleaching out
under an early sun

already hot
on the neck
of everyone

parading onto the plain.
When we travelled
in this territory

at our ordinary speed
we made
20 miles a day

though every hour
we could see
more outcrop basking in the grass.

We rattled across
the stones scattered around
Scotts Bluff where we had to stop

for repairs.
Our wagons were pulling apart
and half the freight fell out.

The Murphys' wagon had warped wide open.
Flour floated thru the floorboards
and collected in a cloud

of white dust
laying down a little trail
everywhere we went.

I listened with dismay
when Jacob said he was leaving
a linen chest.

"I'm sorry
but the damn thing
is so heavy

what can I do?
The spokes are split.
The freight sits too low."

I could say
nothing to my brother
to make him happy;

the fatigue he felt
was under his skin
and wouldn't wash away.

"I can't cart all this crap
and stop to tie it up
and anyhow

it's shabby work
that won't hold together for a week
in wet weather."

I said, "We'll see
no more rain this summer
so why worry?

If you want to bitch
about bad luck I lost a cow
to the cramps after Ash Hollow—

Eddy has no more meat
unless we take time to hunt
while we're here—

Reed has to tighten
his tires and replace
a rear axle and reduce his weight—

for that matter
your foolish Irish
families like the Murphys

would do well to sell all
their livestock and start home, but they won't.
No one will."

We put off work
sitting in a pleasant pool of shade.
Reed fanned up a fire for the coffee

and we watched while two boys dropped
a dozen doves or more
slinging pebbles

like pellets
whistling
in the warm air

wherever the birds were
weaving above the wet bank.
Breen's boy and the big Murphy boy hiked

their pants up on their hips
wading into the water
holding onto

one another's shoulder
while they fought
for support

shoving
wrestling and
locking arms laughing

as they sat down
with a white splash
in the beaming stream.

They stumbled up
onto dry ground
and dug the doves out of the weeds

and the rocks
and wrung their necks.
Then the boys brought the birds in

dangling by their legs,
the head hanging loose
and the limp body looking

like a soft sack
full of feathers for their mothers
to pick and cook.

Then Keseberg was here.
It happened that quick.
We thought he might steal back

to camp under cover of the dark,
but he arrived by daylight
and fell from his horse

holding the rein in his hand
as he found his footing.
His face was brown

from so much sun
but close up
he looked washed out.

"Sip some water
and go slow when you eat."
I sat him down not far from our fire.

He was a tall man who had lost
too much weight and now his coat
sagged on his shoulders and his neck stuck out.

I handed him half a biscuit and a cup
and returned to my friends.
He took a bite

of his biscuit
and said
perhaps to Reed,

"What the hell
are you looking at?
Do you like to see me eat?"

Reed replied
(for my benefit),
"He hasn't paid his proper debt."

Keseberg kept his tongue.
A crowd was collecting
close to the fire.

I wondered, "What
will we tell him
when he's done?

Do we let him
stay in camp
so he can recover?"

Adamant as ever,
Reed was ready
to dismiss my question.

"Tell him we want
no part of him
and run him off."

But when I thought
of our situation
I had to disagree.

"His wife is still
with us. Surely
you know she needs him

and besides
by now his supplies
very nearly

equal yours.
He has equipment
which we could use."

Reed was reluctant
to give ground.
"He can't be allowed

to have his guns.
I won't trust him
with any weapons."

Closing his eyes
Reed raised his head
remaining righteous

as a man will
when he sees
he may be wrong.

I had to laugh at him.
"Jesus," I said,
"just for once

why don't we
try to use
a little sense.

Suppose he will share
his tools with us?
His whole load?"

I waited for Reed
to respond. Finally
he whispered to me,

"Ask him, George."
I walked over
to present my proposal.

He met my plan
with one of his own.
"At least give me a guarantee

that I won't lose
the tools I need.
You can take

whatever you want
if you'll pay for
anything that you break."

I told Reed this.
He felt it was preposterous
to talk of terms

but I believed
the man had suffered enough.
"I want what's fair for all of us."

Reed's reply was,
"George, don't be an ass!"
I called Keseberg over to my side.

"You can stay," I said.
"But your guns are my property."
He pushed past me to find his wife.

Returning to our task, we had to gather
our gear again and repack
the calf-bound black Bible,
the account books, and the almanac.

6
Killing an Antelope

Reed was eager to hunt
and I was willing so we went
to tell Bill Eddy.
"Unless I'm wrong you can use more meat."

"The whole camp could,"
he replied,
and came along.

It was a dry day.
The sun sat smoking in the sky.
We shucked our shirts and piled them in a heap

and filed uphill
myself last, Reed just ahead, Eddy in the lead
after an antelope

who looked lost
and appeared to grope
to find his footing.

He slipped out of sight
until we saw him bounding up a bluff
half a mile off

as if he was floating
more than running
over the rubble

only to arrive
on the top
of a rock table.

His rare eyesight
and his hearing
made him hard to hunt;

we had to hike
higher—then work
behind his back

down a steep slope.
I could grip my fingers on a rock.
but the sole of my boot would slip.

I said, "I guess
I'm too old to keep up with you boys."
We crouched by a wall of shade.

I told Eddy,
"If you see a shot don't wait."
He propped himself on a rock

and I reached his rifle up
while Reed and I remained in the shade
hearing that slow stride

slapping the brush below
not timid at all
not even troubling to be too quiet,

leaving a thicket to stare
for a moment into the light.
The sun was a hot shawl on his silky hair.

Eddy got a good shot.
I saw him leap
and stumble.

We raced down and found him
flopped on his back
writhing around on his spine.

He was sandy brown.
A full-size buck
with a big phallus,

his snowy belly blowing out
and horns plunging in the grass
ripping the green ground around his head.

His legs scissored in mid-air and froze
but both his horns
tore up the turf.

"I've seen enough,"
I said and Eddy
loaded and fired.

I helped haul him in
and his hide felt warm yet
as we trussed him up for the teamsters to quarter.

We washed down with cold creek water
and toweled off and returned
to the slope to find our shirts.

On the way Reed and I
saw six coyotes creep closeby
sniffing over the ground for bones
before we ran them off with ringing stones.

7
We Visit a Village of Crows

Below the bluffs
we drove with a dry wave of dust
whirling around our eyes
until my mare

leaped uphill
outrunning the rest
and trotted down and found the river

much to the surprise
of the women wading there
rinsing and wringing out their clothes . . .

squaws of the Crows
who rolled up their dresses and invited
the sun to warm their thighs

while they squatted in the shallows.
As Reed arrived behind me
one girl grabbed the garment

which was hitched over her hips
and a wet moon marked her hem
when she shook it down.

Our party approached—the women
waited in the water watching us.
Then it was only a matter

of minutes until we met
the most remarkable man
I've ever seen . . .

A Crow rode between Reed and me
bringing us a bow
honed out of horn

taken from an elk
and decorated up and down
with rings of brown and red.

In turn we gave him two bolts
of cloth and a little whisky.
It was plenty.

He wanted us to follow
on foot until we reached a gully
which hid their homes. I remember his hair

was pasted in a stiff pompadour
though in the rear it flowed to his feet
where it was dragged in the dirt.

Claws clung to his shirt as if they were charms.
A cloak like clean snow drifted down his back,
and birds made of beads were sewn on the skin.

. . . At the edge of his village we saw more
than a thousand horses penned in a corral
of criss-crossed poles. A Crow stood guard

by the gate with a rifle in his arms.
Then we entered the town. The large lodges
towered above us and appeared as white

as our canvas covers but they were made
of buffalo skin stretched in the sun.
From every door we heard dogs bark

and men emerged who wore robes of elk
which the women had rubbed so soft
that it looked like linen.

Their chief lay sleeping in the shade
of an ash tree under a river
of raven hair. Over and over

a girl groomed his hair by sweeping it
around her wrist until it fell
in a black lake on her lap.

We watched her dip
her hand in a bowl
of bear grease and begin

kneading it into his hair
without waking him
and combing his hair

the length of his spine
with porcupine quills.
Well, we walked on

and met more white people
from a previous party
milling about the village,

men who decided to stay
an extra day because of the buffalo
grazing near here—

thirty or forty strays
left behind by the herd
when the Crows accomplished their summer kill.

Reed and the rest wanted to hunt
but by now I felt indifferent
so I said to Reed,

"I'll watch you shoot
but I'm too old
for the sport."

Anyway I went
with the other whites and perhaps
ten men plus two boys

from the village each of them
equipped with a quiver
and a short bow.

Soon we found
the buffalo feeding
in reach of the river.

I hung back and learned
the Crows liked to flank the herd
however small it was

and select a single cow
to give chase to
and shoot it in full stride.

Reed's method was more direct.
He rode down a cow blindside and shot it.
I saw him kill six the same way.

Each one when it was hit
lumbered on a little and stumbled
onto its knees and made a dusty mound.

Reed was really elated . . .
"Wait until I tell Margaret," he cried.
"My God what a marvelous day!"

The Crows hacked off the hindquarters.
We helped tow a cow over on its back
and cut it from the throat to the tail.

Then we slit along the leg to the hoof.
A rope harness was rigged to my horse
and we tugged the hide inside out.

Reed said, "If I were in your place
I wouldn't let them put my mare
to such hard use."

While we worked a boy rode down
on a bull but it turned
and his horse balked.

He flew into the air
and tumbled to the ground.
He tucked himself in a ball

as his horse kicked dust
around in rings and trampled
on his ribs

before anyone fired.
We came to carry him away
and rode him home roped over

Reed's mare. Then four men
lowered him outside the door
of a certain lodge.

His breast barely rose at all.
A small blood spoor
formed on his mouth.

Someone sent for a shaman
who appeared with a pack
of boys disguised as bears.

They crawled on all fours
while he shuffled his feet
among them and sang

the healing words
that we could not comprehend.
His body was concealed in the skin

of a brown bear
including the cumbersome skull
but in place of paws

he wore bracelets
which were the wing-bones and claws
and beaks of small birds.

While he was singing and moaning
at one point he had to bend
and scoop a gourd of water.

He paused like a priest
about to anoint the boy
but he poured it onto the dust.

We stared at the splattered mud.
The boy lay dead.
His father and a young friend

hauled him home to prepare
the body for burial
and the family for mourning.

We were led away and kept busy
visiting with other whites.
It was almost night

when we were sent
to the house of our host.
By then the smell

of wood smoke and warm flesh
floating around the room
turned my stomach

but I managed a smile
in front of his friends . . .
big-boned men who were very vain

about their clothes . . . They sat
near the flame to unlace their leggings
and stroked their robes

as they joked and talked
taking bites of broiled meat
and fat from a bowl

rinsing their fingers in turn
and wiping them clean
on a heavy pelt . . .

men whose hair was so long
that while they ate it fell in folds
on their feet by the fire.

And since no one felt
frightened now we spoke
nonsense not knowing the correct

words and Reed and I
feeling the effect
of the haunting atmosphere.

Over us a dozen or more
scalps dangled from a ring
and as if they were

stalked by a ghost
the black paws of a bear
circled in mid-air.

We sat up late with our host
and drank his whisky and like fools
we walked out looking at the sky

on a summer night when the moon
which is the favorite fob
of madmen was hung high
in heaven, lighting all the hills.

8
Drinking with the Crows

Some bear sat here
and rubbed my hair.
In short, I fell asleep.
But who waltzed away with my shirt?

The night's as cool as a hole.
Cover my heart my poor
naked heart with your hand

whoever is there, there!
The tall weeds are all awake
with a woman's walk

and what is her wish,
will she whistle
into the bush?

Will you?
O, if you do
I'll come to you

just as I am,
as bald as a bird
as clean as a clam.

Some other sound sniffs around.
A black weight crashes
thru the grass.

When he bends above
my face his cold
kiss feels like a frog.

All nonchalance and nose
and the hair of a hog.
Is it a hound halfway

out of hell? Is it you?
Do you suppose he knows
I'm a long dog too?

Who held my hand
and stole my coat?
Here's no man's land.
Don't let bears vote.

9

The Hour Was Late

At Fort Bernard our teams were shod
and Reed's wheels
required iron tires
but he complained,

"The merchants in this place
will tell you
to pay the price

or go to hell.
We have no choice
so they gouge us.

I hate to be a sucker
and let them all pull
my pockets out, like a fool."

We purchased what we had to
and after dark we fed
a slow fire

with the wood
of the sage nearby.
The sparks rose over the riverbed

as we spoke with the people passing
from west to east
going against the sun

morose men mostly
who abandoned their ambition
and were heading home to retire.

But one was a trapper
called Jim Clyman
and he remembered Reed

from years before
in the Black Hawk war.
When he heard that we relied

on Hastings' book
he sat on his heels
drawing trails in the dirt.

"You never saw
the salt desert
or you would know

you don't want to
drive livestock
without any water

or so much as
a handful of grass
and if you ever get across

you must haul your household
to the sink of the Humboldt river
and over the mountains

with a tired team . . .
if it's all the same
go up to Oregon where you can farm

or else go home
but I think
California is out of the question."

To this I replied,
"We're aware
of the mild weather

people enjoy there
and the best books promise
that settlers are sure of success."

He said, "I know
John Sutter, the Swiss,
has built a fort for himself

near the Sacramento
but when you live that low
a cold fog comes with the rain in winter.

And the mountains will see six months of snow.
Last year the Sierras were white
for weeks after Easter."

Reed said we were sorry
to hear he had been
so damn disappointed

by what he found.
"But we'll proceed
to Bridger's post

just as we planned.
Hastings is waiting
to show us all

the rest of the trail
that we're to take
until we arrive

in California
at summer's end
and select our land."

His friend suggested
the reliable
trail to Fort Hall

but Reed remarked,
"That way is not
the nearest route."

Clyman would say
no more on the subject
so Breen brought a bucket

dripping from the river
and doused the fire.
The hour was late

as I lay down
at the door of our tent
wanting to sleep

in the net
of the night
where we swim

within
the limits
of our liberty

like any creature
which is caught
in this life,

a far-flung web
of darkness though
it was woven with the stars.

*

Soon dawn disturbed
the brown arm
of the water

and sent insects
rustling across the grass.
We got to our feet and set out.

We drove for two days
shuttling thru a dry summer breeze
before we saw the white adobe walls

of Fort Laramie.
The foundations of clay
were completely finished with brick.

A blockhouse had been built behind a fork
of green land where Laramie creek
sweetens the silt of the Platte

and in the intense heat
when one wall allowed a little shade
some Sioux slept at the foot of the fort.

Their dogs
jogged down to where the water joins
and there by the alder bushes we undressed

to bathe in the quick current
soaping our skin and scrubbing our clothes.
Then we laid our laundry on the alders to dry.

Everywhere a pair of black britches
or a white frock was folded
across a sunny rock.

I watched Eliza
trying to whack the water
flowing past her and shivering with laughter.

I gave Georgia
a pony ride upon my back
sitting down

now and then
to dunk her like a duck
while Tamsen held Frances looking on.

We dressed again
and had to hike uphill to the fort
where we spent the night near the gate.

The following day was the 4th of July
which we chose to celebrate with a feast
of fresh meat!

Then we moved out
and it was another week
before we arrived at Independence Rock

like a lifeless whale
upon the ground,
the grey hide

of the huge stone
bearing the names
of many people carved in its side.

From the site
of this landmark we left
for South Pass and on the peaceful banks

of the Sweetwater
we let our livestock eat
wherever they could come to grass.

We began to drive
over level land
where no trees turn the wind

until you see the willows which shade
the Little Sandy creek
whose warm banks

resemble a beach . . .
the ground itself is like a bog
soaked by summer rain

and the grass within reach
was trampled under
hundreds of hoofprints;

the parties that passed us
had encouraged cattle to graze here.
Their tracks travel toward Oregon and disappear.

In our own company a dreary debate
arose about our route.
For all of those

who were dissatisfied
this was the place to separate . . .
Some were set

on the short-cut
which we intended to take
thru the Wasatch

and the desert beyond.
Others were unable to decide
because Clyman

had tried to tell us
not to abide by the book.
So they said,

"We ought to heed his advice.
To hell with Hastings
if we can save

time and trouble
going to Oregon
and not run any risk."

At a meeting that morning
I was elected the leader of our party
and I announced,

"Hastings is a guest
of Jim Bridger
at his post

so we will have
a guide
we can trust

for the rest of the trip
but you can quit
if you like."

Many people preferred
to form a party
for Oregon

or try to reach
California by Fort Hall
which was the longer route

and so they said farewell
—perhaps half in all—
and they drove off.

Though old friends
were still on hand
we were sorry to see

the others leave.
My wife was
worried and she

hid her face and wept.
"Don't be afraid," I said
and kissed her.

We watched
the wagons wallow out of the sand
and onto firm soil.

Then we turned
our own teams
southwest and we drove for days

over
the dry ground where not one leaf
let its shade

fall to earth
and the wind in which the dust arose
gave no relief

until we came to a clump of cottonwoods
at the side of a creek.
A rotting rail fence

staggered around a patch of land
which was Bridger's post.
The door stood shut

against the dust
drifting under the fence.
It gave way from within

and two men met us—
a white and a Mexican
who let us into the store.

In one room I saw
blankets and bear skins
laid out on the same tables.

Long loops of rope
hung above bins
full of new nails—

loaf sugar was for sale
and crisp canvas covers
and even the antlers over the door.

Outside sat a smokehouse and stables
where waves of dust
washed past

our wagons waiting
while the wind troubled the ground
like an unprotected pond.

Bridger had gone
to trade with a tribe up north
they said. He might be back in a week.

We were welcome to stay
if we could pay
for what we ate.

Hastings was away
on business.
When he heard this

Reed replied,
"We are his business.
He should be here to lead us."

But we were told
he had hired out
to a previous party

in which there was
such harmony
that little time was spent

on argument
so they made
remarkable speed.

"But here we are!"
I cried.
"What are we to do now?"

"Since you came this far
why turn back?"
the Mexican said.

"Follow his trail
and as you reach
the Wasatch mountains

you might meet him
at the stream
on the way in."

We bought beef
and made repairs
and bedded down beneath the trees.

We departed at daybreak
driving to the Weber river
where our bad luck grew somewhat worse

for we found nothing but the grass
bent back and the incessant sound
of water swishing under the aspen boughs.

Hastings had left
a note attached to a branch
like a large leaf.

            I plucked it off
            to read the message.
            "He says the route

            that they cut
            into the canyon is so poor
            we can't use it.

            We're to wait
            in this spot
            until he returns."

            No one was satisfied.
            We expected to be
            led to safety

            and learned instead
            that our guide
            had gone on
            and we were alone.

Book Two

10

Cutting a Trail

McCutchen and Stanton and Reed
galloped up the green path
to overtake the guide.
We kept a quiet camp

by day—sunlight shook
the heartshaped leaves
of the aspens. The dark

that filled the small sky
walled off by woods
brought us no sign

of the three men
until one evening Reed rode in
to tell us, "Hastings' route

climbs up the rocks
and our mounts gave out.
I bought a bay

off a preacher in the party
driving to the desert.
McCutchen and Stanton

have stayed behind—
they can't find a soul
who will sell

a horse or mule.
I took time
to blaze us a trail

but it's bitter work.
What's worse, we lose
two weeks breaking brush

in the canyons
and hopping across
a web of creeks."

By now we could not
turn back to take
the established trail

so we tried to cut
aspen twice as tall
as his house wagon.

Down in the narrows
men had to chop
with axes and picks

thru thickets of willows
and wild rose . . .
Breen complained

about his back
and mine hurt too.
"I'd rather keep up

than stop to eat
in the shade," he said.
"If I quit

the pain begins
to split my spine
like a blade."

However we did
stand admiring the land
while the women would rinse

our shirts and every time
Jacob's oldest son
let the sweat run

from his blond beard
as he halted there
in a trance. He left

his hand on the haft
of his axe and stood
staring up the slope

where he was to cut
but his mind was gone—
a man may see a valley

overgrown with trees
or a simple stream
struck by sunlight

and in the cave of his chest
his heart falls
because he loves

the land too much with his eyes
and he feels unneeded
he is jealous

of the generous nature
of all things whether
they are large or small

vegetable or mineral
and the wild life
and the long lights of space

so he cannot
move on nor come
deep into the place.

                              *

We cut for nine miles the first week
and the blue thorns that sprout like stars
under the weeds made my hands bleed.

I stood in the gloom that gathered
on the bank of Bossman creek
to see a wagon crawl toward our camp.

The wheels wobbled away from the frame
where a row of ribs was visible,
and the high hoops had been blown bare

leaving little streamers still attached;
the breeze flapped the canvas like a tattered sail.
Soon we saw that this skeleton did not arrive alone.

We quit work and while we watched
two tall wrecks which rattled louder
followed in the uneven wake of the other.

Three altogether and all
owned by Billy Graves
an old farmer from Illinois

who got down gingerly
jumping into the grass;
the fleece on his face

seemed to be sewn
to his jaw-bone where
it grew as grey as wool.

His wife and also
his married daughter Sarah
had a helping hand

from Fosdick
his son-in-law
who lifted them to the ground.

Then we met Mary Graves
a straw-blond girl
still unwed though

a handsome young man
hung at her side.
He was John Snyder

a driver about
20 years old and
a favorite of her father.

With the addition of these people
our party swelled
to more than 80

far too many
for practical travel
unless they were willing to work.

Snyder's neck
was a mound of muscle
that looked like a yoke

and all week with a pick
he would pull up rocks
that could break my back.

Fosdick helped by hauling water.
But some men slipped into the shade
or tried to hide in a field of phlox.

Ba'tiste was the first to make himself scarce.
"Where in the name of God did you go?"
I asked him at dusk.

"You said you knew the route
when you signed on . . .
It's too late

to regret those lies
but I'll tell you this
if you want to eat you'll have to work."

People used a meadow like a public park.
When Wolfinger the wealthy German
strolled across the clover

hand in hand with his wife
his shirtsleeves would shine
as white as the wings of a swan.

A man by the name of Antoine
who was paid to keep
his eyes on the cows

was often gone
from dawn to dark
and never seemed to miss his sleep.

Then one night sitting at supper
where the campfire
increased the heat

in her red hair
Breen's wife Mary
made a cruel remark—

"We must suffer
so much on account
of one man's mistake!"

and she meant Reed
who rose in anger
and walked away.

"This is unjust," I said.
"If it weren't for him
we couldn't see

where to clear
the trail and we
would be helpless here."

She wiped her hands on her hips
and went on: "I don't care
what you say

you're no fool
but everyone knows
you follow your friends too far.

What good are the maps
that you find
in a book

which is blind?
Reed rides off
to see the guide

and sees him off
for the desert
to direct a different party

folks farther ahead
who pay him very well perhaps
but why

are we digging
in the damn canyons
by ourselves?

Three weeks
we will waste
on this wicked trail

which is the work
and the pride
of James Reed.

I think we were
stupid ever
since the start

to put such faith
in the word
of any man

and you can tell
your friend
to go to hell

though it won't do
any good of course,
he'll take the wrong route

by mistake again
and end his days
at peace in paradise."

Mary grew quiet and grinned
glad she had said
what was on her mind

and then Stanton led
McCutchen toward the fire on foot
limping because their boots were busted out.

Their feet bled
and their shirts were torn
to shreds by thorns.

Amanda handed her baby
to Margaret Reed and ran to greet
her husband . . . I brought the other man

to Tamsen and she dressed his sores.
He took some tea from a tin cup
and later he was able to swallow soup.

*

That week we cleared 12 miles of trail.
When our wagons faced a wall
we spiked the wheels with stakes

and ran long ropes from the axles and ribs
to pulleys on the top
and together towed them up.

I trussed my last mare in a sling
and with Ba'tiste clucking in her ear
five of us pulled her a foot off the floor.

As more men leaned on the hoist
the horse began to float
in the warm air

rising
while her legs went on rowing
nowhere

and she felt
the silence pass underfoot;
then the ground arrived and the high grass.

At times we were less successful
and the bay that belonged to Reed was lost
in a long fall.

. . . We came
to a final rise and everyone agreed
upon a single method

for the oxen were almost dead
as they fell on their knees in the shade.
I asked Ba'tiste to bring me the best.

We double-teamed to draw
30 wagons full of freight
over that height

and let them roll
down the green slope
the ribs rattling all the way

into the welcome meadow.
From here a great lake was in view
and the sun grew gaudy on the water.

A range of mountains rose on our right.
And in the distance dead ahead
glittered the brilliant brow
of the desert as white as snow.

11

We Bury a Man beside the Lake

We found forage for the cattle
in a lush field
which was fed
by fresh springs.

Standing there
we were able to see
how Hastings' trail reached

far away
grinding the warm grass
and entering an arid plain

where the thin ruts of the wheels
appeared to be etched
in the ground

beyond Black Rock
a square of stone that made a box of shade.
The only dark object anymore . . .

a solitary marker
high as a house
on the south shore of the water.

When we left
for that landmark on the next day
you could hear the grass whistling in the heat

and I ordered our daughters to sleep
if possible or at least
stay under cover.

Nevertheless
we lost one
person from our party

an old man
named Halloran
a consumptive who had almost

choked on his phlegm.
Tamsen washed him
and toweled him off

while I made room
in our wagon
to put him to bed.

Both my wife
and Elizabeth
kept watch by candlelight

but late at night
the blood bubbled in his mouth
and long before morning he was dead.

We waited until the whole camp awoke
then brought the body
to be buried

as sparks of the sun
burned out on the lake.
A crowd collected to view the corpse.

A piece of paper was found in his pocket.
I examined the note
and told my wife,

"It seems
that he wrote a will
leaving his money to you and me."

Breen and Billy Graves
had to see for themselves.
I showed them the paper as proof

and took the key
to unlock a trunk
where the deceased hid his savings.

Over a thousand dollars in all . . .
We hired Snyder to dig a deep hole.
It was hot work and the shade was small.

Since the dead man was a high Mason
Reed thought it appropriate
that he perform

a ceremony
while the body rested in the pit.
Then we shovelled the salt over it.

Still the crowd was slow to dissolve.
The same men remained by the rock
though no one wished to talk.

I leaped onto our wagon
and stood on the seat.
"Listen to me!"

Everyone looked up.
The children made walls with their hands
around their eyes.

For the adults
shawls and hats
shaded their faces.

"We won't survive without help,"
I said. "No one
can outrun this sun

if left to himself.
I mean no man
acting on his own.

Help one another.
Share your water.
If a man feels faint

that's all right
let him ride inside
so we keep close together.

And as a rule
we'll try to travel
only at night.

We cross moist ground
almost marsh land
for two days

to arrive
at the salt flats—
from that point drive

the livestock
in sight of the wagons
from dusk to dawn.

The surface of the salt
should cool down
and we'll find our way
by the light of the moon."

12
Betrayed by Our Books

Hastings nailed up another note
in a region which had the damp
air of a swamp—here and there
it was pocked with pools as deep as wells—

but birds pecked this paper from the post
before we appeared and several scraps
wafted off to fall among the weeds.

When we found enough pieces to form words
Tamsen put them in place like a puzzle.
Her face lost its color

as she turned to whisper,
"It's twice as far as he thought.
We'll drive for two days without water."

How were we to account for this mistake?
Nowhere was it written in his book
or any book we brought

that this could occur.
Not in Frémont's work
nor the unnecessary

botanical library,
nor the friendly almanac.
Nor the family Bible for that matter.

Bewildered we began
to hunt for every vessel that we owned,
every barrel or jug that could carry water.

From well to well we had to haul
our buckets and fill the kegs until
the wagons whined under the added weight

turning toward the desert
where the warm day declined
and the sun lay level with our eyes.

Men grew weary of the effort
of looking away from the light
and then it was gone and dusk came on.

We welcomed the cool curtain of the night.
Graves gave out with a song.
The Murphys joined in.

Among my friends the talk picked up
and for a time we felt like singing too.
Yet we seemed to be entering another trap.

In the glow of the moon
we saw the silhouette of a mountain
unmarked on our map.

It loomed like a wall
and I told the teamsters to stop.
"We all need sleep."

Keseberg was quick to argue.
"You can make camp
or keep going—

take your choice—
but we know the sun
on the desert

is too strong.
If we stay with you
some of us will die."

Even old Graves disliked the delay.
"Why do we have to drive
in the heat of the day?"

Tamsen tugged at my sleeve.
"Tell them you were wrong,"
she whispered and I had to climb

on my perch to explain:
"It was my plan
to drive after dark

but that was a mistake."
People crowded in
like cattle in a pen

except the enemies
that Reed and I had made.
They remained at the rear of the crowd

to sow distrust
with their whispers—
Keseberg and Spitzer and others—

until talk of leaving
flowered where the friends
of Graves were huddled with their wives.

To stop this sort of trouble I said,
"If we separate
we invite disaster.

Keep together
and tonight
enjoy your sleep.

Can we cross
that range with no more
guide than the moon?

Think of the loss
of our stock alone
if we start

up a steep slope
when the cattle are
clumsy and full of fright!

They can't climb
without enough light
for safe footing

so wait for morning.
The sun will feel fierce
to some of us

but we can rest
and the teams too
if we watch our water."

This promise to protect
life and livestock
impressed my listeners

and I asked
them all at last,
"The men who say

you must hurry on,
will they stop and help
if you break down in the dark?"

No one cared
to answer my question.
I dared the opposition at its worst

but it was mainly
persistence I think
that persuaded people.

I simply talked
the difficulty to death
and when I stopped
the crowd dispersed.

13
Land Logic

Slowly we descended on the west
slope with the sun
in our eyes
and prodded the poor cattle down the rocks.

We were happy to set foot
on the desert after dark.
Children chased each other into the night.

When they raced back in the moonlight
we built a fire and a circle formed.
Some whisky was found.

Stanton strummed a banjo.
In a minute Mary Graves
and Sarah were singing.

Snyder danced with her.
Others added their voices.
I lifted my daughter

Eliza and we trotted around
the flames. Before
we finished though

a chill crept over us.
I spread our blankets on the sand
which sparkled like an autumn frost.

Then men and women began
to bed down on the cold ground
that did not hold much comfort any more.

                              *

              At dawn we saw the waste
              around us in this place—
              no bush or tree anywhere.

              We started to work
              our way between bunkers
              and over the baked dunes.

              Travel was slow. The bulk
              we were bringing broke
              the crust beneath us

              and it sapped the strength
              from our teams to pull
              thru the soft sand.

              Reed and I
              at length lost sight
              of the lighter wagons

              ahead. We had to unload
              our freight. Iron book ends
              and bolts of cloth not worth

their weight now, kettles
and copper candlesticks
and a brass bed-stead

of Jacob's which stood
upright and glowed
in the white heat

as Eliza pinned a sheet
onto the frame for other
travelers to discover.

Like Margaret Reed
Tamsen abandoned
her favorite footstool.

We left a chest made
of oak. Whatever we could
throw out that wasn't food.

Then we gained speed
and soon we hit
the salt flats

and drew near
the rear of the train
where our friends were.

Our faces and hands
turned white as
the fine salt left

a pall upon our skin.
It powdered my beard
and clung to my shirt

where I was wet.
My wife wore it
all over her skirt.

It stuck in our sweat
and this was what formed
a white film even

on the sunny flesh
of children. It gave
our little girls

a ghostly color
as if they had gone
beyond the grave.

And at this stage
we were afflicted
with strange visions.

I met Bill Eddy
standing alone
at some distance

from where his infants
and their mother took
cover in their wagon.

"I saw one man," he said
"and then an entire line
that looked exactly alike.

They walked for a mile
in step with me—
about two dozen in all.

I stared at the face
of the nearest one
and it was my own!

Then I just stood still
like a man made
out of wood.

Well, they stopped too.
They would repeat
every gesture of mine.

I raised my hat
and they lifted theirs
at the same time.

I was convinced that the heat
of the sun had done
damage to my brain.

And I was afraid
that I would grow insane
and die here in hell.

I raced for our wagon
and found my wife
and buried my face

in her breast.
Because I was
with her and

no longer alone
my mind grew serene
and so the scene vanished."

We could explain it merely
as a mirage but I was
not ready to disparage

anything Eddy had said.
It had the ring of truth.
Other men saw an image

of the complete train
accompany them in the heat.
Always it was parallel

and always there were people
who were recognizable,
it would seem. There was never

any devil nor the gaze
of the dead who come
to surprise us when we dream.

Whatever we saw or thought
we saw by the sun's rays
reflected in fact life

which was already there.
For example Foster's exact
likeness of his large wife.

One man saw his horse
appear in the thin air.
Whether it was our wives

or a mare that seemed
solid enough to saddle
in the mind's eye

it was only the play
of light on our senses
but I could not conceal

my own fright for it made
men almost mad to see
illusions look so real.

The next day the party
prepared to enter
the desert sink—

a bog or marsh
of salt water
lying in the center

of the dismal land.
From the start our wheels crushed
the surface

and settled in
but people pushed on
over the slush

while it filled with water
in our tracks.
Cattle collapsed

and died.
We had to halt
only halfway across.

Eliza complained
of a cruel thirst
and wept for anything wet

to soothe her throat
and shrink her tongue.
We wanted to share

what well water remained
but soon there was none
and no one dared to drink

the dull liquid that drained
in warm pools by the wheels.
However we couldn't bear

to see our daughter suffer
unable at last to lick
her lips. To make

their mouths wet
their mother gave the girls
sugar to suck.

"Save some for tomorrow.
We won't find water
any sooner than that."

When one boy felt faint
a bullet which had been
hammered flat was put

behind his teeth
so that the metal
might moisten his mouth.

The wagons crawled away. I watched my friends
driving a lighter load increase their speed
but Reed and I were inevitably slowed

because we had to haul the weight
of his house wagon besides our freight.
Some cattle feeling the slush underfoot

simply settled down and were dragged to one side.
They were too dried out to go farther.
Reed decided to search for water . . .

He was younger,
and his mount was stronger
than any horse of Jacob's or my own.

He told Elliot,
"I want you to bring
the wagons with the cattle.

When they're no longer
of any use in the yoke, let them loose
and drive them after me to find a spring."

*

On his way he passed a boy keeping
a lookout, a little embarrassed
by his sister's weeping.

A woman seated in the dim
shade of her wagon shivered
like a deer as she stared at him.

A girl walking
swiftly in the heat
was waving her hands and talking—

All these people were left behind
once the men unyoked
the cattle that went sun-blind

on the salt and set out to seek
water far away in the hills
where the desert ends near Pilot Peak.

Every mile he had to pass
dozens of cattle dead
from lack of water or green grass.

At the place where Eddy shot
his horse the stiff
carcass was starting to rot;

the meat had begun to stink
in the breeze while the sun
scorched the sink.

Then he felt the salt flats
underfoot and saw men run
after their cattle, whacking their hats

in the wind, turning a cow that swerved
toward any scent of moisture.
Finally where the desert curved

against the grassy slopes he arrived
at fresh springs. From our
friends in camp there he contrived

to exchange his horse, and with four full
waterbags he came back
on the crowded desert at nightfall.

Cattle rumbled past him and soon
he saw more men on foot
trying to head them home by the moon.

He heard the hard ground vibrate
beneath him as the livestock
thundered thru the darkness, and late

in the night he rode by
the wagons he had seen that morning.
They were moving out under the cold sky.

Among all these he could not find
one of his own . . .
His house wagon waited well behind

the others and Reed didn't know
if his wife was there
with the children until he saw

Margaret emerge from within it.
She said, "The oxen have fled!
All of ours are missing. The minute

they were unyoked they broke and ran
and every one is gone.
We must walk in from here if we can."

The Reeds walked until they lost hold
of each other's hands and fell
on the sand. For shelter from the cold

that flooded the floor when the wind swept
the surface like a crust
of snow, his children slept

among his dogs. In a ring around
them all the animals lay down
in the dark. Seconds before the sound

entered their ears they felt it. A rumble
below their blankets. Drowsing,
they saw the dogs begin to tremble

and suddenly a steer
who was wild with thirst
threw them to their feet. Everywhere

the dogs backed up to bark
but he reared around
and scattered them in the dark.

No one was awake
in Jacob's wagon when they overtook him
at daybreak.

We made room for them to ride
in our wagons all the next day
and on into dusk as we walked outside

looking for the sign of a campsite—
the fires that sparkle and shine
like the stars floating in the night.

*

By dawn when we reached the springs we counted few
cattle grazing; with so little livestock
we had no use for freight wagons now.

Reed was reduced to one ox and a cow.
For a fee he found he could borrow two
oxen from Breen, bringing his team to four.

The teamster Noah and I rode once more
into the desert. We transferred Reed's food
and clothes to his house wagon as he had planned.

We saw that we couldn't dig deep in the sand
without salt water hissing into the hole,
so we made a cache on top, in this way—

In one wagonbed we were careful to lay
all items of value: silver pieces, plate,
even mantle clocks. Then we shovelled a mound

of sand over the pile. At sundown we wound
away toward Pilot Peak and returned to Reed,
hauling the hulking wagon in our wake.

"This is everything you told us to take,"
I said. "I don't see how you'll manage
Margaret and your children." When we were thru

there was no room to ride in. "Will any of you
haul half our food with you?" he asked us all.
"I'll pay you for whatever you can carry."

No reply. No one offered. It was necessary
to make some portion of his food available
to the people he approached, or leave it there.

"We'll take yours with our own if we can share
the use of it," said Graves. "But your money
is worthless here. You shouldn't even ask

to purchase space; we're running all the risk.
Why should we want to have your wealth
when there are no stores, and we need to eat?

Has it occurred to you that the weight
of your food and our supplies is sure
to tire our teams? Why should we die rich?"

So the family of old Graves gained much
of Reed's provisions for their own use.
A paper was drawn. In this way they were paid

to transport his food. Finally, in a trade
made among friends, Eddy who had lost
his one wagon was anxious to arrange

a shelter for his children in exchange
with Reed for two oxen. While this was done
dusk came to cool the grass, we settled down

to supper by separate fires. In the crown
of a cottonwood a few stars flickered.
The tongues of our flames licked at the dark.

In time, our talking floated up like smoke
and mingled with the chatter of the leaves.
But the night unnerved us even as we spoke.

*

Music like the low waves
that lap along a lake
when a breeze weaves over the water

glided thru camp. It grew
first from the family
grouped around Graves

where he watched his daughter
in a loose gown undo a pair
of red ribbons and let down

the hive of her hair;
a honey-heavy light fell
over her shoulder like a shawl.

She waited for a glance
from her father and felt
one foot forward, then stepped

into the surf of the song,
as if at a sign. As if
the old man's eyes made her dance

a circle with her sister
Sarah Fosdick, her face flushed
by the fire. He was wary

of the men who admired
the light on her long legs
and dreamed in the dark

but he sang himself and seemed
content when Snyder came
to take his turn with Mary.

And since his singing blessed
the couple they embraced
and kissed.

We found a fiddle.
The girl slipped free.
Clapping filled the clearing.

Against the darkness
Mary whispered
something out of hearing.

Leaving the listening
shadows once again
Snyder approached the fire.

His walk was awkward
then for his legs
moved more like logs.

He hiked his pants
and tried to dance
as well as he was able

reeling from side to side
where we made a ring,
anxious not to stumble.

The agile girl could glide
as nimbly as a needle;
in and out of the light

she swirled as her gown began
to billow in a circle.
Sweating he stood

and coughed in a cloud
of dust while Mary came
to meet him in the middle.

Though he seemed stiff
in every joint
Snyder beamed and bowed.

Slowly he unbent,
but at that point
one member rose—

Mrs Murphy said, "Good God!
It makes me so damn mad
when a man sits and stares.

If a grown girl shows
how her breasts swell up
the size of ripe pears

and she rolls her rump
around like a melon,
you won't turn your eyes

to anyone else. It always goes
that way. Oh I realize
many are married, and old

and tired, and all but buried.
So you are out of luck.
All you dare to do is sit

dreaming about it
while the young fellows pluck
the fresh fruit.

But for other people
it isn't so simple.
Like any decent woman

I'm careful of my name.
I fear the Lord.
I teach my sons a sense of shame.

Still, I'm only human
so when I work hard
I want my reward,

and I'm no silly goose
though you may think so.
I know my mind. You watch.

If a bull breaks loose
I won't get gored.
You'll find me up in the crotch

of the closest tree."
She shook her hair
and her voice flew like a flame

as we heard her scream . . .
"What's a woman to do?
Even more than most,

I admire men. But when
you swagger around
to me at night and boast

about your parts, I'm bored
to tears," she said
although she didn't look it.

Just then the dancers
saw their chance
to disappear and took it,

fleeing from their friends
by the fire to hide
uphill in the shadows.

"Where did they go?" she cried.
"Well God bless them!
And it serves you right!

No woman wants to work
all day and sleep all night.
That isn't what we need.

But what hope is there here?
You gape like ghosts and crawl
along with so little speed

in your limbs that you look
like you've swallowed lead.
On the day when I see

my friends once more
I'll tell them all
I've come back from the dead!"

As she turned from the laughter
of the younger men and fled
in the dark they followed after.

I started to stand.
But Tamsen put her hand
on my leg and said,

"Stay where you are,
you stiff old steer!
So I sat down and we all sang . . .

While Stanton hummed
he banged on the back
of the banjo for a drum.

Denton drank the last
of his liquor and let
the mouth of the jug

slip from his lip.
A little more spilled
into his beard

and the young man yelled,
"What the hell's the use—"
and dropped the jug in the grass.

Children took it up
like one of their toys
tipping it and trying to

toss it back and forth.
For a while Jacob's boys
wrestled and rolled

in the dust like dogs
and sat up and howled.
The entertainment ended

the moment that we heard
another noise. There was
a hubbub among the animals,

a queer series of squeals.
We scrambled downhill
in time to see an ox

tuck his legs and spill
onto one side. An arrow
quivered in his hide.

We saw no one but I suppose
the indian knelt nearby
in the night where he took cover

watching what we would do,
waiting for us to go.
He had time to draw his bow twice.

A second shaft was lodged
in a lame horse.
But what was worse

than the loss of that ox
from the paltry total of our cattle
was the pervasive hatred it created—

our dread that every digger
indian hereafter was a sign
of danger. As old Graves said,

"It was some God-damn
filthy diggers
hiding behind a rock.

They squat and shoot
at our livestock
without any fear

of attack; when we try
to drive them off
they sit in the darkness and wait

until we leave—
knowing that we'll leave
the dead animal here.

Then they can butcher it
and carve whatever meat
they want to eat and trim

the bones and hooves
and carry the carcass away
piece by piece like a pack of wolves."

*

We crept beneath our quilts at Pilot Peak.
I tossed all night, badgered by our bad luck.
I prayed we had seen the end of it. But no . . .

We woke to find the Peak was wrapped in snow!
Its dome wore a cap of fresh fallen snow.
Its flanks were wrinkled with crisp white creases.

I saw the dismay in many faces
and heard the fatigue in my friends' voices.
The advent of autumn was an unhappy omen . . .

We were weeks from California, and someone
must travel to Sutter's settlement
on the Sacramento river and ride back

with provisions. Flour and dried meat. On pack
horses or mules. "My wife's a sparrow,
she has no hips," I said, "she has no shadow."

Ladies laughed at this. I added, "And we know
our little ones are too weak to go on
eating like lizards." I spoke at midday

as the sun crossed over us and dried away
a fine-spun frost . . . Stanton and McCutchen
on plodding mounts set out for Sutter's place.

The sun scorched the sky and still a trace
of snow remained upon the peak. We kept
our cattle grazing by a running pool.

A week passed, the water every day was cool
and clean. On most mornings the sun seemed slow
to warm, the grass looked glossy with moisture.

We wanted only to rest, at this juncture.
Seeing the snow, no one wished to look back
on our bad luck or talk of it anymore.

Reflection only led us to deplore
the sudden end of summer and lament
the time we wasted in this trap. Whole days

spent unloading. Stupid disputes. Delays
caused by the cattle roaming or Hastings' wrong
advice . . . We were warned that to survive

we must lay up grass and water for a dry drive
of two days. Which meant at worst we might
travel a day and a night—where we instead

wandered a week in the desert and left dead
a third of our herd of cattle. Add a third
of the wagons abandoned, still it doesn't explain

all the destruction done. We could never regain
the time taken, or our goods or livestock left
on the salt. But this was not the only cost.

There is a land logic which we lost . . .
A sense of the likelihood of new terrain
to sustain us. The same logic that lives

in our blood, telling us that bottomland gives
promise for planting. Or for example,
the simple certainty that we would find

spring water among rocks when the sun reclined
on green slopes gleaming like good pasture.
But we hurried out only to discover

a prickly patch of greasewood growing over
the dry soil, white with alkali . . .
Nothing in nature was what it might seem!

The promise of finding forage by a stream
proved false as well—both banks were bare
although the current there cut swift and deep.

We lost the last advantage which could keep
our company from harm. It was this sense
of the land that had departed in a dream
while we went on like souls that are still asleep.

14

One Day near Dusk

One day near dusk I left camp to look
for a place to piss in a clump of cottonwoods
whose paper leaves had gone from green to gold.
Not far from where I stood I thought I saw

something stirring in the grass—a dog
shook himself in the shade perhaps
pestered by a lively lizard, or the breeze

fluttered a few leaves. But when I took
another step closer I was able
to see someone sprawled beneath the trees.

He lay flat on his back. I saw the face
of our good friend Breen, and I was afraid
poor Patrick probably drove himself to death

searching for shelter where his wife would not
complain about the hot sun, and even
the blessed birds could communicate with heaven.

Perhaps he suffered terrible stomach trouble
from the fried potatoes that he ate. Or he might
have been brought down by a severe snakebite.

Then I noticed how his hands held his Bible
all but motionless and I finally perceived
that he was simply sleeping with the black book

propped on his chest as though a huge crow
crouched upon his shirt and lifted
its wide wings in rhythm with his breath.

The red sun achieved a brilliant glow
and small birds sang in the slants of light
while Breen slept as easy as the dead.

Since he was safe and I of course had other
business anyway, I hid in the shade
only a little longer and then returned
toward our camp feeling suddenly relieved.

15
The Division of Day and Night

Crossing a flat valley
at our level pace
the 18 wagons make
15 miles daily.

Each crossing brings the teams
to good grass by the springs;
in a meadow mountain sheep

crop the grass
but antelope keep
to the high brown slope.

After a long climb down
from the hunt at mealtime
the roasting meat starts to smoke.

Then the dusk comes
dragging the cold across the rocks
above us.

Three weeks into September
the leaves change color
and clutter the grass.

In the almanac this date marks
the sun and moon brought in balance
at the autumn equinox.

Aspen lose their leaves and stand
bone-white while the heavens
divide the hours, day and night.

The sun displays the earth or stars
barely illuminate the sky
and we who inhabit the land
go equally in dark and light.

16
The Law of the Land

Later there was little game
to provide more meat
and nothing occupied our time
except to listen for the snakes

sliding under the sagebrush
which had gone grey in the heat
of the summer that was over . . .

We had to realize
we would starve unless relief came.
So one evening I called

the members to a meeting:
before we were to arrive
at the Humboldt river it was clear

we could never cross
a thousand miles of dry basin
and mountain ground

extending from here
to the Sacramento valley and survive
without fresh supplies.

"Someone must be sent
to Sutter," I said
but they remained silent.

Reed was not about to abandon
Margaret and the children
in their poverty

nor Eddy either
his family in need of food
and no one else as competent to hunt.

Who would trust Keseberg or his friend
Reinhardt to return?
Or Spitzer? Of the rest

Billy Graves was reluctant
to leave his father.
Snyder was busy with their teams.

Fosdick and Foster
didn't offer
and Breen was absent.

In the end
Stanton and McCutchen
volunteered.

At dawn
we gave a big bay
to the tall young man

and a sorrel to his small companion
and said goodbye and be careful
and wished them well.

Stanton left no people
in any worse peril if he failed,
and McCutchen's love

for Amanda and their child
was reason enough to believe
that he would be back.

Slowly we began to break
camp and continue on the tiresome trail
to the Humboldt river.

Early in October
as we approached an apron of grass
growing upon the bank

of the brown water
everyone could smell the stink
of the mud moving by

in this bitter river
without beaver or trout
which we would follow

for three full weeks
until we saw it settle
in the slough of its sink.

We wanted our oxen to eat
the thin grass every day
to sustain their strength.

And while we travelled there
we were still a party—
a convenient community

in which each person gives
a portion of his independence
to the total group

in the hope
that he will share
in the progress of the whole—

a company which willingly conforms
to a particular code
of conduct that includes

travelling as a train,
by which I mean
remaining in line

during the difficult stages
although rotating
the order of driving of course

so the leading family on this day
tomorrow falls to the rear
where the dust is worse.

One morning climbing a hill
in single file we came
to a dead stop.

We remained at a standstill
while the wagons
of the Graves family

were drawn down the slope.
Snyder took them one at a time.
When he was tired of waiting

Elliot pulled up
with Reed's wagon to pass
the one ahead.

He had the misfortune to flick
an ox belonging to Graves
and the animal broke

into his own team.
Two oxen tangled
and locked legs and fell

and cracked a yoke
and snarled all the lines.
Snyder went at them with the blunt stock

of his whip
beating them both on the skull
mad enough to kill

both beasts
until Reed arrived
and wrestled him off.

Whether it was one
he bought from Breen
or Bill Eddy

no one could say
but the situation was the same
in either case. You could hardly allow

an animal to be injured
and absorb the loss
when you had no way to replace it.

Reed said, "I demand
that this man
make good the damage."

The driver replied with his whip
by bringing down
the blunt butt

on Reed's head.
It cut deep
into his scalp.

The blood ran
onto his brow.
Reed drew his knife

and Margaret came
clutching at his shirt
in time to take

the second stroke.
She slumped to the ground
where she lay stunned.

Reed stuck his knife
in Snyder's breast
and the blade entered his lung.

The young man fell in the dirt
and all his friends
flocked to his side. Mary among them.

Patrick Breen was there to say a prayer
and hold his head in his hands
the moment he died.

Virginia Reed ran to remove her mother.
Her father seemed to be dazed
and blind with blood

as he stood motionless
and let the other men surround him
and bind his wrists with rope.

He was led away
from the dead man
without saying a word.

Everyone walked down
from the hill in the direction
of a wide meadow

on the north side
where there was a stony place
to ford the river

and here his case
was tried by a collection
of his peers.

No lawyer could deny
that Reed killed Snyder
but Bill Eddy spoke

of the necessity
to consider the question
of provocation.

"He has no cattle.
He lost everything he owned
on the desert—

his large wagon
his last piece of furniture
and every other possession.

There isn't a man
among us who has lost more
than poor Reed.

So when he saw
Snyder beat the animals
unmercifully

moved by sympathy
and thinking how hard it would be
to restore his team

he intervened
and he was clubbed
like the cattle.

Before you blame
Reed please realize
what caused the crime.

If the wild wrath
of that youth
resulted in his death,

Reed was not responsible.
Remember the horrible harm
that was done to him

by the beating—
the blood running
into his eyes—

and his desire
to avenge the blow
which wounded his wife.

To do him credit
we must admit
that many men

in such distress
would act the same,
and we should be forgiving."

Graves disagreed.
"Nobody
will be satisfied

if we pretend
to be God
whose glorious mercy

is a mystery.
A dear friend
of ours has died.

It's our job to see
that justice is done
to the living."

In front of the crowd
he turned toward
his daughter Mary

who wept
at the side
of her brother.

No judges were chosen
this time. Instead
all the adults

who possessed property
whether it was a wagon
or only livestock

were invited to decide.
After Graves had spoken
the vote was taken.

A wide majority
of the members found Reed guilty.
Some said that he ought to be hung.

Keseberg raised the tongue
of his wagon into the air.
It was a stroke of ingenuity.

He discovered by using a yoke
beneath it for a brace,
with Reinhardt's help,

he was able to lock
the beam in place
and make a gallows.

Milt Elliot thought
he was at fault
and said he was willing

to lose his life
if that was necessary
to let Reed go free.

Old Graves objected.
"Reed's the one
who needed a knife."

Sending Sarah to wait
with the other wives
who sat on the stones

above the water
but would not look
at one another

or their husbands either
Fosdick took the side
of his father-in-law:

"All our lives
aren't worth a damn
if one man

is larger
than the law of the land.
If Reed can kill

to preserve his pride
how do you propose
to prevent the slaughter

of the rest of us?
When he goes
unpunished

we'll make
a joke of justice."
Then he gave way to Graves.

Holding the hand
of his daughter
the old man raised

a final question
concerning our friend:
"I have to wonder,

in this man's mind
is Snyder worth
as much as an ox?

If Reed thought so
why didn't he report
the brutal attack

on his animal
which everyone saw
and bring us together

to sit as a court
to take testimony
and punish the guilty,

after his hearing
in a fair trial first.
Isn't that how it was done in the past?"

Reed remained silent and allowed
Eddy to plead
in his behalf:

"Is he to hang
for using his knife
to defend himself?

Look how he was hurt.
Look at the blood
here in his hair!"

"That doesn't matter,"
Keseberg answered.
"The question is

whether a man
who is arrogant enough
can take a life

by his own hand
and pay no penalty
for committing the crime."

Eddy had nothing else to say
by way of argument
and the attention

of everyone swerved
again to the gallows
where the rope was ready.

It appeared that the party
would proceed
on its own authority

to execute Reed.
Elliot left the low ground
along the river

and returned with a rifle
for himself and one for Eddy
and the gunsmith Denton came with them

and these men were
swift to surround the prisoner.
Then Elliot began to bargain.

"I don't care
what you believe about Reed
you can't claim

he killed Snyder
in cold blood.
Let's be reasonable.

If he's guilty
the penalty
must not be death."

In front of a gun
Graves was willing to back down.
"It's possible

we may have gone too far.
To be fair
his punishment

ought to be banishment
with no weapon
or food of course.

Simply treat him
the same as
in Keseberg's case."

Keseberg was angry.
"I don't see
any similarity.

He persecuted me
for playing a prank.
No one died

because of what I did
and I don't think
you'd set him free

if you weren't afraid
to face his friends."
His rope remained on the gallows

but the Graves family
felt more flexible.
They were ready to let Reed leave.

So he was helped
onto his horse and allowed
to say goodbye to Margaret.

Meanwhile the crowd
clattered across the gravel
going back from the riverbank

to see Reed ride away.
Two men kept watch all day.
When dusk arrived

the sound of relief
was like a little rain
that rustled over the ground

and those who slept
awoke anxious to travel.
Twelve wagons wheeled out once more

holding close to the Humboldt river
in hope of having grass nearby.
Twice a day we stopped

to minister to our blisters
or let the livestock drink.
Nevertheless there were people

who could not keep pace.
The man by the name
of Hardkoop was one.

An elderly Belgian who fell behind
the rest of us and became
a casualty.

When his boots wore out
his feet blistered badly.
He paid Keseberg for space

where he could ride in his wagon.
Then the owner changed his mind.
It wasn't that he had no room

but he didn't want the extra weight
so he put his passenger out
and left him there

and went to the whip
hurrying his team
while the old man beseeched him:

"As I'm a Christian
like yourself
take me in!"

Our teamsters told us this
on the following day
when it was too late

to return and fetch him.
Because he was alone
no one had missed him.

After dark more misfortune struck.
A digger snuck in close to the cows
and showered them with his arrows.

He was shooting purely
for his own pleasure
and to see how many he could hurt

in the same spirit
that our boys had enjoyed
slinging stones at the prairie doves

when we were in camp
back at Scotts Bluff.
However we could hardly afford

the loss of all these cattle
from the tired herd . . .
We didn't discover

the attack
until daybreak.
Many of my own stock

when they had been hit
wandered onto the stones
and staggered into the river.

Here and there a cow
who still wore the arrows in her back
stood bleeding in the water,
no good to anybody now.

17

Our Suspicions Are Aroused

One evening
the wealthy Wolfinger was missing.
His wife was talking
with Elizabeth

when it first occurred
to anyone that he was gone.
I left the women

to feed the fire
and ration
a small supper

and went to ask
where he might be.
My teamster had the answer—

Ba'tiste told me
he saw the man drop behind
to keep company

with Keseberg
and his less prosperous friends
Reinhardt and Spitzer.

It hardly sounded safe.
While no one wanted to alarm his wife
I feared we would find

Wolfinger's corpse
unless we went
after him in time to prevent disaster.

As we set out
a stream of stars shed little light
on the dead land

but we barely started
when we met Keseberg coming
in to camp.

He assured everyone
the other men were merely
five miles back and driving slowly.

We decided to return.
We settled down
with Wolfinger's wife to wait

for her husband to arrive.
The stars passed
over our fire

hour after hour
until the sky to
the east grew grey.

By dawn still
he had not come in,
and she was hysterical.

I called upon
the young men in the party.
"Who will go and look?"

Billy Graves took two
friends and left
to learn what had happened.

He returned within the hour
only to report,
"We found no trace of Wolfinger.

His wagon is in order
but the team has gone
grazing somewhere or they were driven off."

No sign of the missing men.
Later in the day
Spitzer wandered in

to say Wolfinger was slain
no doubt by the diggers who lived
like dogs in the hills.

This was one of the men
who helped Keseberg plunder
a funeral perch long ago on the prairie

and now he couldn't explain
where Wolfinger was
(or Reinhardt either)

but no one was willing to delay
longer for the widow's sake
on suspicion alone.

So we let her think
Spitzer's story
was true, it was

the damned diggers who
killed her husband for his money
and hid his body,

and we invited the widow
to join us and ride
inside with our children
for the rest of the journey.

18
A Strange Study

When we reached the Truckee river
we turned our teams
loose by the water
where the grass grew thick

and would provide
sufficient forage.
In the meadow there

we made our camp
and a quick supper
consisting of coffee

some sugar
and not much more
until the evening

when Stanton returned.
With him were seven mules
sent by Sutter

supplied with flour
and enough dried beef
for all to share.

And at his side
rode two indians
named Luis and Salvadore.

They were herders who worked
on the low land
around Sutter's Fort,

silent young men
who had copper skin
and short-cropped hair.

We were given to understand
that they spoke Spanish
but I don't know,

and just how much
these two understood
of our own speech

we never learned.
Luis and Salvadore
weren't very verbal.

With white people
they liked to use
as little English as they could.

When asked why
they kept so quiet
Stanton said they were worried

about the mules because
Sutter swore that if one was lost
he would hang them for their trouble.

So they seemed unwilling to talk.
Nevertheless we were impressed
by our new guides

though it should be said
that together they made
a strange study.

Neither one was blessed
with a large body
but obviously

they had crossed
the Sierras safely
and they could lead

our party now
by the same route
that brought them to us.

However we knew
it was treacherous
to travel at all

if it started to snow.
We planned to pull out
as soon as the stock felt fit.

Meanwhile Stanton sat
by the flapping fire
talking about the trail

which twisted off
over the meadow
and continued to the lake

approaching the pass.
Tamsen held
Georgia who was cold

and Eliza sat with
her aunt Elizabeth.
Jacob and Eddy

and Margaret Reed
with her daughters
Virginia and Patty

and Amanda McCutchen
who was sleeping
in a blanket roll

and Wolfinger's widow
and our Ba'tiste
made up the rest.

When Amanda awoke
to find Stanton back
and McCutchen missing

she started screaming
but he assured her
that her husband lay

in bed at Sutter's Fort
where he fell sick.
Regardless of his size

his illness left him
too weak to travel
but he would be along when he was able.

When she heard
he had not died
then she could bear

his absence in silence.
We had no concern
that he might desert

the party or his bride
and their baby—everyone
felt certain that he would return.

*

Again we grew
preoccupied with the need
to repair our gear.

In the mountain creases
men noticed new traces
of snow that did not melt

but our oxen were worn to the bone
and the meadow remained green
so we stayed

for four days
while the cold came on
and we let them eat

until one morning we found
the cattle fractious
as though annoyed

with the weather
and they wouldn't nuzzle
the nubs of grass when the first snow fell

during the day.
They preferred to avert their faces
from the flakes.

Once the sun
dissolved this snow
we wished to break camp

since it was necessary
to round the lake
and climb the pass

before a storm
might seal it shut,
if we weren't too late.

I sought to secure a team
by talking to my friends
and finally calling

on anyone else to negotiate
a fair exchange,
trying to trade

for six oxen strong enough to pull
their own weight.
While I stayed put

my brother walked
from one wagon to another
inviting the owner over to our fire

where pewter and silver pieces were displayed
and my wife and I might arrange
the appropriate notes.

Most men weren't willing
however to barter
for an animal

and it was the middle of the night
by the time I could acquire
suitable stock.

But very soon
we were left with little sign
of the party itself.

If a half-hearted restraint
had held many members together
it vanished like a shadow

in the dark
where each man could see
his own life

was in danger
the longer he delayed.
Graves and the guides and all the rest

decided to depart.
The last transaction was finished
and we were at work

packing our possessions
by lantern when we heard
the wagons slip out of the meadow.

Most of the party
were prepared to go
without us and for now

there was nothing we could do
but listen to them leaving—
our teams not yet in the yoke,
our horses helpless in the seething snow.

Book Three

19

Shelter in the Snow

At dawn we were awake
and hurried out
to catch the others who had gone
ahead to the lake.

I looked for
the fine lines left
by their wheels

in the shallow snow
and they were easy to follow.
A few flakes skidded by in the wind.

Ba'tiste steered our team down
a slope by tacking
this way and that way

to reduce the grade
but the oxen lunged
and the wagon gave a weird roll.

The front end tilted and fell
and we cracked an axle on a rock.
When we stopped it was as though

we had dropped into a hole.
I climbed into the wagon and found
Eliza lying stretched out and stunned.

I held her quiet in a quilt while she revived.
Then her mother took over
and began to rock her in her lap.

Her color crept back
and we saw no sign of shock.
Later we let her have a little snow to suck.

Jacob's boys
combed a creekbed for kindling wood.
I cut a lodgepole pine

for the new axle
and after it was stripped
so the grain was accessible

I said, "You want to be careful
to plane the end in a clean circle."
Then Jacob went to work with his chisel.

I was watching when the blade buckled
and ripped a flap of flesh
from the roof of my hand—

I howled and the blood spurted out.
I saw the vein pour up,
and the blood showered down like red rain

as my wife ran to my side
to hide my hand in her blouse
while it continued to bleed.

She asked Elizabeth
for a hot cloth. When it came
from the flames it was white with steam.

She rolled the skin in place
and wound the cloth around.
As the blood soaked in

a red stain spread over the top.
To stop the pain they stuck snow
in rags and wrapped the cold packs

on my hand until it grew numb
and I felt nothing
at the end of my arm.

After the axle was set
we started up.
My wound was slow to thaw

but when it did the pain
would burn so hot that I cried
while I walked beside our wagon

afraid to faint and feeling sorry
for myself and all the time hearing
the wheels slide in the low snow

as we moved into a mountain meadow.
Some white trees formed a column there.
A creek crawled between the aspen

and the water looked clean
in the cold glow of the afternoon.
We led the oxen in

among the bright trees standing
about the brink where they stopped
and leaned over and drank and drank.

While we waited I heard
a single shriek, and then silence.
It wasn't the spiral call of a bird

which seems to reply to itself
but the cry of an animal as if
it had been caught by surprise.

Jacob took my rifle and we went
looking for any kind of small game.
I worried that the surface snow

was too old by now. We saw
a leaping line where a hare
had left his tracks. And nothing more.

Under some alders as we came
along the creek we found a fox
scratching and scratching in the snow.

Jacob raised the rifle and took aim.
His shot flipped the fox off the bank
in a backward arc and he fell

head-first into the water.
We fished him out and I took hold
of his legs letting his fur drip

over the snow while we walked back.
We chopped off his head with an axe
and set him to roast on a spit.

The meat was awful—it was like
the sometimes sour or bittersweet
taste of tree bark—I coughed up

my mouthful on the snow in disgust.
While others ate, the sky grew dark.
At the same time it became clear

we must make camp and prepare
to spend the night. All around
the snow began to whine in the air.

Our teamsters pitched a pair of tents.
We built two huts out of aspen boughs
which we tied together.

To make a roof we used the dried
skins that we had on hand
and spread a wagon cover over the top.

When we thought it was watertight
we brought our blankets inside
to wait for the storm to stop.

The flakes fell all night and left
a wall at the entrance
to our hut

until I dug us out
of the drift.
Then I joined Jacob

standing in the snow.
"Look at this.
The cattle can't find any grass."

We beat bushes back
to look for forage
and while we were at work

we saw two men approach the creek
from the direction of the lake
lifting their legs high

fighting the deep footing.
Reed's right-hand man
Milt Elliot

and Noah James
who worked
for Jacob when he had his teams

came from the camp
that the others had made.
I asked Milt what it was like.

He told me
they arrived at dusk
and pushed on past the pines

and had to pause
where the sedge grass grows in the water.
People pulled back

and kept their wagons together.
They slept among the trees.
A cold wind whipped the cattle.

But by dawn it died down
and men thought they might
manage to drive

the length of the lake
and up the mountain in daylight
and across the pass.

From there the two
indians could guide
everyone else to Sutter's place.

He said, "If we got thru
we meant to outfit a party with mules
and come back for you.

So we stamped our boots
and trampled the snow to free the wheels
and shoved the wagons out of the woods

and slid them onto the shore.
But the best oxen
were useless to us,

you couldn't yoke a team
and whip them over the snow.
They were too weak to work anymore.

Each driver had to stand
hip-deep in a drift
and whack his stock ahead by hand.

A guide who had hold of the long
handle of a spade tried to goose
the mules to lift their legs loose.

We left the wagons stuck
on the shore and inside
we hid the quilts that we couldn't carry.

We tied two blanket rolls on the mules.
While I prepared my pack
Keseberg rode by on his horse.

Then the others started up.
When Breen's cattle balked
he cursed them onto the slope.

Wherever we walked
the older children followed in our tracks.
The smaller ones were riding on our backs.

At first you climb around the rocks
and trees that rise from the snow.
When we had hiked halfway

we were sweating like horses.
The water poured off our faces.
Our clothes were soaked regardless of the cold.

I couldn't see the summit
or the pass near it.
Then we simply stopped.

We fell out
along the frozen slope.
Far below us the lake glowed

and all we could do was gulp the air
with our mouths wide open like dogs
bursting for breath.

I tried to move my feet
but the muscles in my legs
felt as tight as a knot in a rope.

Stanton took a guide with him to scout
the white banks up ahead
but they wallowed back

bringing bad news.
Snow sat five feet deep in the gap.
It choked the pass from side to side.

We had to decide
to burn a pine
and remain where we were

or begin our descent in the dark.
Foster felt we ought to return to the lake.
Eddy said to wait for daylight.

It started to snow.
Margaret Reed knelt next to me
and we lit the tree

which went up like a torch.
We brought our blankets into the glow
of the tall flames.

I remember hearing
the snow hissing
as I fell asleep.

Then in the morning
the guides were missing.
Foster believed it to be a trick.

His wife Sarah
thought so too.
'They brought us here by design.

You see how they've run
up the mountain
to watch us die.

Soon they'll come
to take what we leave.
That's the way they live,' Foster said.

I disagreed with him.
'For Christ's sake
use your head.

What do we have
that anyone
would want to steal?'

This put an end to our quarrel.
We could do nothing now
but retreat.

Using my belt
I measured a drift
which was ten feet tall

and those ahead
appeared higher.
So we went down

the same way we came
though more careful
in the clean snow

and in time
we set foot on the shore
where we saw

no one near
the wagons which remained in a row
alongside the lake.

A crust as fine as frost
clung to the wooden frame
as we walked up to the last one.

At the end of the line it loomed
like a large coffin covered
with a canopy and set on wheels.

The bedclothes which belonged
to Margaret Reed
were stored inside

and we were about
to fetch them out
of the rear when we heard

a noise as though
someone had snored.
At the sound of our voices

the two guides rose up
to open the canvas flap
trying to wipe

the sleep from their faces.
In the snowfall
the two men

had drifted down
the slope together
and spent the night under cover.

I told them to carry
the quilts and come along
and we walked into the woods

behind the lake.
We had to hurry
and cut enough pine

to build a shed
and finish our work
before it grew dark."

We were worried
about Margaret Reed
and I wanted to know,

"With her husband gone
how can she provide food
for her family in this snow?"

"At least twice
this week she has bought
horsemeat from old Graves

and she sent me to see Breen
about the carcass of an ox.
While we talked

Breen raised his price,
but he won't sell many.
No one else has any money."

After the first snow
the livestock at the lake were starved.
Milt said the place

provides scarcely any feed
for cattle. A little lupin
and leafy green mule ears

and some mint but not much good
grass can grow
under the pine trees.

Already the men have carved
their horses and quartered the mules
and set the meat in the snow to freeze.

When I heard how this had been done
I took him by the arm and said,
"Tell me about the others."

"Spitzer is sick.
The rest are all right so far.
Even the infants

and young mothers
like Amanda McCutchen
or a girl like Mary Graves

or an old man like her father.
And Fosdick is there
and Foster is with his wife Sarah

and Mrs Murphy
and the young man named Dolan
and your friend Stanton

and the gunsmith Denton
and Keseberg of course.
Is there anyone I didn't mention?

People keep indoors day and night
so the camp is very quiet.
Breen reads his Bible on his knees.

To make a carpet for his floor
he spread pine needles everywhere
and when he prays he kneels on these.

Most people settle for two or three
walls with a wagon cover on top
or any shelter that they can contrive.

Keseberg's wall leans against Breen's.
Mrs Murphy and her sons
have hung up an ox hide

that they use for a door.
If the snow will melt
and unplug the pass

I think we can survive
and make an escape
before too long.

A little of our old anger
is buried now," he said.
"Graves and his family and Margaret Reed
all are living in the same shed."

20

When the Children Were Asleep

When the children were asleep
Tamsen took my hand
and dressed the wound
with a clean cloth

while I held my breath.
The pain was swelling
far up my arm.

She opened her blouse.
"Look at this,"
she whispered.

"You can count my ribs—
Feel here and press
your fingers in."

She unpinned her hair
and shook it out
so the auburn braids

dropped down her spine
and seemed to steam
against her skin.

When she turned her breasts
were as pale and cool
as wax. She whispered,

"Look how my hips
hardly hold a skirt
in place anymore."

As I joined her
in the blanket
on the pine floor

she made a remark
about the slack skin
that flapped on my legs.

She liked to see
the way they shook
but I told her,

"If it's a matter
of their shape surely
yours look better."

She laughed lying
in my arms with
my hand at rest
on her small waist.

21
We Bury My Brother

Night after night
the cattle wandered into the woods
or fell down in deep drifts
on the open meadow.

We couldn't construct a pen in the snow
so it wasn't long
until they were all gone.

One morning we went looking
for a large ox
that vanished in the dark.

As we hiked along the creek
and the sun slipped thru the trees
together we came

into the thicket,
a cluttered place
where the snow was thatched with bare branches.

"I need to sit for a minute,"
said Jacob.
I asked, "What is it?"

He said, "I feel sick.
Here, please
help me with my coat."

He was in a sweat
as he sat
and scooped a handful

of snow
and scrubbed his face
and rubbed it on his wrists.

I said, "You better
go back and
let Elizabeth put you to bed."

He wouldn't listen to me.
He got to his feet.
"Let's try

one time
while we're here
and see what we can find."

Ponderosa pines
with a plated bark
like a turtle's back

lay in the snow.
Aspens bent over, bridging the creek.
Dead trees decked the banks with their boughs.

From the debris we trimmed
a long limb to poke like a pole,
probing for cattle frozen under the snow.

So much snow flew in the air
that I spit it off my lips.
Then I heard

Jacob yelling,
"O Lord, my legs!
My legs! I'm going in!"

He was trapped in snow to his belly.
I hollowed out a hole around his hips,
sweeping snow away until his legs were free.

I helped him over to his hut.
He ducked thru the door.
"I'm done for today."

"Goodbye," I replied
and set off
to see my wife.

We knew now
we could not get meat
from the cattle wherever they were.

However I had
something in mind
if we could find a few good hides . . .

Elliot told us how
the ladies at the lake had learned
to make gelatin.

Hold some strips
of hide between a pair of sticks
over a fire

so the flame singes the hair.
Then drop the bald hide
into a pot

boiling it
for a day or more.
Then dip your sticks

in the pot, like spoons,
and lift them up
and lick the pulp.

Or else pour
the jelly in pails
to freeze and keep.

But neither of us could rip
a single skin loose
without leaving a hole

where the snow would fall in
so we gave it up
and went to sleep.

In the morning Elizabeth sent
one boy of hers
to say Jacob was worse.

We had a little beef broth
about as weak as tea
that Tamsen had hidden away.

I brought a pot with me
and went to see Jacob.
I found him lying on his back

stretched out in his black coat
and too near death
to take nourishment.

His pulse whispered in his wrist.
When he died at last
we carried him off to the creek.

I laid our Bible aside
and assisted Ba'tiste with the spade.
We dug a pit and put Jacob in it.

Milt made a wooden marker,
two pieces of pine
tied in a cross

which he set in the snow
and drove down
with a blow of his fist.

Then I took up
the book to read
but the words were like water

as they wriggled
and wouldn't rest
in place on the page.

I couldn't look.
I turned my back.
The boys led Elizabeth away.

When the corpse was covered we left too.
Worried and short of breath
we walked back to camp.

On the way
I stopped in
to visit Elizabeth.

Her hands hid in her shawl
but her skin hung
on her arms like silk.

"We both know somebody
will bring us food
before too long," I said.

A candle shot shadows around the room.
I saw where her sons sat
in the gloom against the wall—

it cost all their strength
to return to the hut
in the wet snow.

Their lips seemed to shrink
away from their gums
which made their teeth show—

their eyes were almost shut
the entire time
and I think they never saw me
come in or go.

22

A Death-Bed Confession

Sleet hit the hut
and the bare boughs chattering overhead
and almost tore loose
the roof of canvas and hide.

Water dripped down
and made mud underfoot
although we spread

pine needles
over the floor.
I gathered green branches

and built a bed
for my family
and Wolfinger's widow who lived with us.

To keep out water after this
we chinked the holes
in the roof with rags.

Tamsen took my knife
to cut up a quilt if we needed more
but by now the roof seemed secure.

However we worried
about the poor health of the Wolfinger woman
and set her near the door

and built a blaze outside.
By the firelight
I discovered

the dark tissue,
the discolored skin
on her fingers.

We removed her shoes.
Her toes too
had been frostbit.

While we knelt
over her in the heat
huddled in the door hole

Ba'tiste crawled past
the three of us
and slid into the hut feet-first.

He stood up
in the low room
his breath blooming

over the small ice
balls that caught
like burrs in his coat.

He had something to say
to me and my wife
and waved us away from the widow.

"We just found Reinhardt.
Noah and I
thought he was dead.

He sits in the snow
and holds his hands in his lap
and stares straight ahead

at the trees.
I think this sleet woke him up.
Imagine that!

He swears he's alone
and he can't feel
his hands or feet."

Before I said to bring him in
I asked Ba'tiste,
"Did you take his gun?"

"No. Does he have one?"
I led him by the arm
across the room.

"You'll have to feel him for it.
But do it," I said,
"or he'll kill you."

"When the widow is awake,"
he said, "I'm afraid
she'll remember Reinhardt's face."

"Just bring him here.
Then if we have to
we can take him to Jacob's place.

But don't worry about her.
She's sleeping like a bear.
She won't hear anything."

The sleet had quit when I looked out.
"Do you need any help?"
Ba'tiste shook his head.

"He's so skinny
he won't be hard to carry."
They brought Reinhardt to the hut.

One went in back and one in front.
They lowered him on the snow
and slid him thru the door.

When they let go
he flopped around the room
flinging his legs on the floor.

I was afraid he'd kick
the widow in the back
but she rolled over in her sleep

and he saw her face
just as we pulled him out
thru the hole to the firelight.

I sat on his chest—
wanting to keep the weight
of my knees on his arms—

but behind my back
his legs quivered like snakes.
He squirmed from side to side.

The fire glistened on his face.
He began to move his mouth
and I bowed my head to listen.

He said in a soft voice,
"I helped to kill
her husband.

Do you remember
when we dropped behind
everyone else on the Humboldt river?

Me and Spitzer
worked together
and we took Wolfinger.

His wife was riding
up with yours.
No one was near us.

I wrapped my belt
around his throat
and fired one shot.

I cut his moneybelt
but Spitzer got
his watch and

we split his gold.
We laid his corpse across
his horse and rode off

half a mile
behind a little hill
and hid him in the brush."

At length Reinhardt grew calm.
A coma left him in a listless state.
When he relaxed his legs didn't shake.

Before the widow woke up he had died.
We dug a shallow grave near the creek
not striking solid mud

below the snow.
Soft snow which we smacked down with the spade.
Then we crawled back inside.

Later we had to steal out at night
and dig him up to remove
what we could for meat.

Arms and legs at the start.
Then the heart and all
of his liver as well.

We would not have done this
but it was so long since anyone
had eaten a meal.

When we returned to the hut
my wife was weeping
and I told her,

"I suppose
he lost his life
to no purpose,

but in this way
if we share his corpse
he may save someone else."

Some nights the air froze
our tracks and
preserved the prints

where our boots sank
down in the drifts
going to the graves,

but these were buried
when the wind arose
shrouding the creek

blowing oblivion over
the low shrubs
and snapping the aspens.

So we ate
and went to bed at night
and awoke in the morning

seeing the surrounding mountains grow
remote and insignificant
the vague slopes

never dissolved
but disappearing
day by day in the omnivorous wind.

Even the large pines
that stand out
like landmarks

here in the meadow
were lost in the easy lambence of the snow.
The only permanence is in our past

where the prairie withdraws
while winter forms
a wide quiet with so little color
that the covered shapes feel familiar.

23
Christmas Day

We decided to say it was Christmas Day.
Living for so long shut in
by the deep snow it was impossible
for people to keep track of the date.

How were we to know?
But we could estimate we were drawing near
to the end of December

and we wanted to celebrate the holiday.
On the morning that we chose
daybreak brought us a sky full of flakes.

They flashed past
our doorway like leaves
when a wind storm strips the trees . . .

A snow that clings to clothes and makes
its own way into the smallest holes
and seals light out of the hut.

*

Eliza lying in her quilt
with her eyes alert
for anything moving

on the floor of the hut
quick-handed caught
four mice in the morning.

We cut off the tails
and heads and tugged
hard to pull out

the   tangled entrails
from inside the trunks
which we cooked up at once.

There was enough for
each person to squat
on the floor and eat

several small strips
of this flesh while
it was still hot.

We were very careful
to save some meat,
and when it grew late

in the dim afternoon
we sat down again
for a second meal.

Finally all our food
was gone. And then what
I did I might explain

if I admit my mind
was sometimes unsound.
The pain from the wound

in my hand had spread
like a slow flame
all the way up my arm

and it clouded my brain.
When my head was light
it was a chore for me

to walk out very far
or even try to talk
clearly anymore.

But when I saw our food
was gone, I stood up
and bowed my head.

I said, "I feel
in spite of the grief
which we share here,

on this the most hopeful
day in the year
we should say a prayer."

Then I prayed, "Dear Christ,
we have seen the worst
weather on earth

and still we live
by hand-to-mouth
and today we want

simply to enjoy
and celebrate the
day of your birth.

We made our mistakes
suffered for our greed
and paid for our pride.

There's no more need
to torment people for
ignorance or guilt.

We have done all
that we can to endure
in this dark hell.

We've paid our price.
And now we pray
for our release!"

Tamsen sat crying
quietly to herself,
I felt like a fool.

I ended by saying,
"We still may hope
to escape alive

if God should change
His mind and wish
to set us free;

if God should care
to see us all
survive . . ."

Here my voice dropped.
I stopped speaking
and raised my eyes

to the solid ceiling,
a dome built
of boughs and skin

sealed fast by ice,
the only holes stopped
with bits of clothes.

It no longer felt
like a cold cave,
but had become

a home to us
and yet I thought,
Good grey Ghost,

winter won't last forever.
The freeze can't hold
too long like this.

So let us see the sun
carve thru the cold.
Let the drifts shrink

down from the door.
May the mild sun
melt the snow away

and free the fields
so that we can drive
across the grass again.

Every night that we sit
in this hut we think
of the green ground.

In our day-dreams
we watch a creek
swollen brown with silt

rise in the spring
while the bank bubbles
and the soft soil steams.

*

In the winter gloom
our girls had grown as crafty as cats.
Thin and grey.

But they were fed today
so we felt content
singing old carols in the cold

although each time
the wind increased
all the walls would creak;

the weight of winter
pressed upon our backs
like a field filled with rocks.

Then the sun went down
and we crept out of the hole
to see the stars,

a million lights
over the lifeless meadow.
We fell on our knees

and crawled back
to our beds once more.
The wind had blown

the whole sky clear
letting the light
of the moon fall
on the entrance like a stone.

24

A Married Man and What He Saw

In bed, lying on
my back I could rise
on one arm
hearing a girl

or the widow say
something unclear. "There's no way
to block the wind."

In a pit outside
the wind rolled the fire over
and it died.

Then the girls
came in
saying the storm had smothered the flame.

"Help me,
put your arms
under me."

They sat me upright.
I felt warm for a time
and then sick to my stomach.

I have no desire
to walk any more.
I sit still or else lie down.

Later
people hiked in
and lit a fire in the pit.

One was Moultry
the same man we heard
had married Mary Lard

        far back
        in June
        on the prairie.

With a few friends
he had come
to carry us to safety.

He peered in the door
and then withdrew,
stopped by the raw smell in the room.

The dung piles
and the yellow stain
of the urine pools.

I sat up. Got up
to greet him
and fell over.

With the help
of Tamsen I was taken out
and seated among the other men.

I was amazed
by the heat of the fire.
It made my eyes water.

We sat there
each of us uncertain how to talk
to the other.

From the lake
these men had found the sound of the creek
and followed it

to our camp
which meant they must have come across
the burial places

broken open
and the evidence of our eating.
Even so

Moultry made the small girls go
into the hut
before he would tell

what he saw at the lake;
our oldest daughter
Eliza was allowed to stay.

His party started
from Sutter's Fort
in the Sacramento valley

outfitted for relief
with many mules
packing flour and beef.

"On our way
we met Bill Eddy
resting at a ranch

in the valley
where he had wandered
looking for food.

He joined up
but most of those
who left the lake with him have died.

We stopped to strap
more meat on the mules
and added blankets

and rode on
above the snow line
where we found poor footing.

The mules broke
their bundles on the rocks
and dumped them in the snow

or rubbed them off
on the trunks
of the pines.

I ordered Eddy to turn back
with Sutter's stupid mules in tow
while we kept on

climbing
on foot
for another week

and made a cache
of what we could
keep from eating.

Then we struck
thru the pass and down the long
mountain face

and found ourselves
walking on the white shore
of the lake.

We reached the woods
on the east end
and at the first

of four sheds
I discovered a patch
of hair and bone."

In each instance he saw
a hedge of bones
above the entrance—

a hole like ours
which is dug down
to the hut below.

The people left
alive are so weak
that any activity is work.

When the corpses
grew too heavy
for the living to carry

a decent distance
into the woods
they kept their clothes

and raised the rest
onto the roof,
where they froze.

They had no more
opportunity to find fresh food
than any of us.

When all the cattle
were killed
or wandered away

and the supply
of butchered meat
gave out

they ate
the ox hides
as we did—

some sixty souls
needed to be fed,
though the figure

is half that now.
The hired hands employed
by Reed have died.

Milt Elliot lies buried by the lake.
And Eddy's wife
and daughter are dead.

One day in December
Spitzer collapsed.
It was Breen who found

that he had gold
coins in his coat
and he hurried to cut

more pine boughs
to build the man a bed
in a corner of his cabin.

Within a week
Breen buried him, but after
the New Year

men dug the dead out
of the snow and took
whatever would make a meal.

Moultry told me
that he passed an hour in the shed
where Keseberg lives.

He saw a supply
of wood and bowls
of blood on the floor.

"He is lame
but he can walk a little.
He keeps a fire

near his door
and broils brains
and other pieces in a kettle.

He'll recover
since he seems
to have no scruple

about his appetite.
He swore to me that he prefers
the flesh

of people
to any other."
All this he said with his eyes

lowered and not looking once
at me, so much as
a glance only now

he raised his eyes
turning around to the trees
and the remains of our meals in the snow.

My face felt flushed with shame
but he was not about
to judge our hunger.

"We had no
choice—" I said,
and perhaps he agreed.

We wondered
if there was a chance
for the children to go

with Moultry's men.
However he had
to explain,

"We want
to help the whole family
when we can.

Another party
will come. Already
Reed has raised enough money

to pay for provisions.
Please remember
there's a limit

to the total number
that we'll allow
to leave the lake.

Some people
are so frail
they can't travel.

We want whoever is able
to walk out
with us when we go

but we must
not take too many:
that mistake was already made."

While we listened
sitting in the snow
Moultry told us how

Bill Eddy led
a large party trying to escape
from the camp

in the hope
that some men might survive
and send help
before the others died.

25

Hunger and Hospitality

Eddy said every person packed a ration
of flour and sugar
and a little beef.
All brought blankets.

The two indians
carried the coffee.
Stanton had come

with them on his return
from Sutter's Fort
and offered to go

as a third guide.
So the party grew inside the sheds.
Graves taught the women how

to make a snowshoe
with the wood of an ox-bow,
crossing strips of hide

back and forth
from heel to toe
and lacing a leather sole underneath,

and nineteen people prepared
to leave the lake
and climb the pass.

Many couldn't come.
Keseberg was lame
and hid himself in his hut.

Patrick Breen believed
it was wise to wait and see.
Most of the Murphys stayed where they were.

Margaret Reed remained
to care for her children,
and Eddy took his family to her door.

He wanted his wife
and little girl and boy
to share the same shed with her.

Then he led the others along the lake.
As the wind raced across the ice
three men quit and turned around

walking in the tracks going back.
The rest went on and bedded down
on the face of the mountain

though Foster complained,
"We won't find dry wood for a fire."
By morning it was snowing. They went ahead.

Stanton couldn't feel much life in his legs.
He fell far back in the afternoon
and was the last man thru the pass.

Old Graves fell asleep
with his head in Mary's lap
and that evening he was dead.

In the morning
Mary went snowblind
seeing a steep green gully

and a stream of smoke
rising from a cabin closeby,
where there was only a canyon covered with snow.

"They're anxious for me!"
She ran off more than once
and slipped in the drifts up to her hips.

The last time she was told,
"You don't see a damned thing.
All you do is dream."

During the fourth day
all the beef had been consumed
and so people sucked on the sugar

as they paused
protected from the wind, waiting
in a sunny cleft

for Stanton to find his way.
He came in on his knees at night.
"I can't climb," he said, "my legs are gone."

By dawn it was plain that he was dying.
He kept back against the rock
when the others started out.

The day after he was left for dead
nobody had any food—
beef or flour or whatever—

Foster went first
and the rest of them followed him
in a ragged line

under the sun.
Eddy said he felt
as if the snow was on fire.

He shut his eyes
and heard the soft noise
of his shoes caving into the crust.

Night found them on a ridge
where they heard the wind
above and below.

Eddy sat down
on the snow and Dolan drew
his pistol from his coat.

"We can't help it.
We need to kill someone for food."
Eddy set one condition . . .

"It must be someone with flesh
enough to feed these people.
Either you or me."

When Foster walked over and announced,
"Antoine has froze both feet,"
they decided to wait.

This man who had herded
cattle for the company on the way was found
to be out of his head.

He passed the night in pain.
It departed and he drowsed all day
in a queer calm on the snow until he died.

Working with knives in the evening
they carved enough to cook
by a whistling fire.

It began to appear
that the loss of more men
might sustain them:

the Fosdicks fell sick
and the Murphy boy was lame from frostbite
and the guides

could not tell
where they were
nor where they were going.

On the ninth day
everyone watched the clouds
passing over the peaks.

Sitting in a circle
they held their blankets behind their backs
to serve as a wall

but the wind
ripped the ring apart;
people let go, the fire flared up.

Eddy said nothing
they tried was any help.
They put on one piece of pine at a time.

The branches burst into light as though they were straw.
The flames flapped like flags.
They spit sparks onto the snow.

A pool formed underfoot from the sudden thaw.
Amanda McCutchen found her legs lying
in the water and crawled away crying.

When the party pulled together
and lifted their quilts like a tent
the snow wove a mound around the wool

and they were sealed inside
where they sat in the dark air.
The Murphy boy died there.

Later Dolan dragged the roof away.
It was morning, on the next day.
The sunlight leaped over the snow

as he stumbled downhill.
The mountainside was ribbed with pine
where he seated himself

to pull his boots off.
He stood barefoot in the snow
and pulled his pants off.

He looked up when he heard his name
but he wouldn't come.
He began to bury his body in the snow.

He was carried up the spine
of the mountain by two men.
Mary Graves gave him her quilt

but he died before night fell.
As dusk came down it was snowing.
No one moved. In the morning

the storm stopped,
and people crept out from beneath
their blankets and the dead

were uncovered for food—
Dolan and Murphy and the herder.
The flesh was fixed onto long sticks.

People were careful to set aside
what meat could be put into their packs.
Foster liked the liver and prepared it for himself.

If anyone was unwilling
he let his eyes fall from the fire
and ate in silence like a shadow.

By now none of the party said, "No—"
Each person consumed his course
and crawled off to sleep in his quilt.

Soon the men had gained
enough strength to go on.
Among the women

Amanda had to be carried;
Sarah Foster sickened and hung on her husband's
                                        shoulder;
only Mary Graves was much revived.

One guide sat stripped to the waist.
The two of them shared his shirt
to bandage their feet.

The party limped out
on the lip of a canyon and came down
ledge by ledge and finished the last of the flesh

on the floor and followed a stream
wherever they heard it hissing underfoot.
Then in the third week

they reached a pleasant plateau.
Patches of brown grass glowed in the snow.
They burned a bush

and took the thongs from their shoes
and singed them in the flame
and chewed them for the juice.

Foster asked Eddy for his gun.
"What good are the guides to us
if we die here?"

Sarah supported
her husband:
"Let him kill them.

Let him shoot
one at least,
so we can eat."

Mary Graves agreed.
"If you will
kill one,

we can feed
everyone else
with that meat."

Eddy kept his gun.
When they were alone
he talked to the quiet guides

and they fled
into the woods after dark.
By dawn a red trail was visible

where their feet bled
leaving the clearing and slipping across the snow.
He said that besides these smears

they discovered the sharp
prints of a deer
cut into the crust—

he walked off with Mary
and they made their way
among the oak trees that grow

at that low height
and the bushes struck with frost,
the thin stems thrust up from the snow.

"Soon we were tired,"
he said. "I sat on a stone
and rested the gun on my knees.

'Have you lost him?'
she wondered.
I answered, 'No.'

Then we saw the oval place
where the deer slept
and we tracked him

into the sun.
We saw how he stopped
to hold

his head erect,
his ears alert
listening for us.

I shot wild once.
My second shot missed.
The third one hit.

'Merciful Jesus!'
Mary cried.
'O yes, yes!'

He slumped in the snow.
We hooted and ran
and jumped on him.

Raising his jaw
we attacked his neck
with my knife.

Letting out
the last life we cut
a huge hole there.

'God bless us, blood!'
Mary screamed and I sank
my arms in the gore.

We drank
by bowing our heads
and licking our hands.

We giggled with glee.
I kissed Mary once
and we embraced.

We kissed again.
Her face red.
Both her hands red.

We pulled out the innards
and sat chewing on the strands
and I hugged her

my hands sticking
to her hair—
when we laid down to rest

I propped my rifle toward heaven
and fired a shot in the air
for the others to hear."

*

People cleaned the carcass
of the deer for two days more
and when they left

their stomachs were stretched
from fresh venison.
Still they staggered

like seven lunatics
until they stumbled onto the trail
of the guides again.

They followed it down
among the foothills where the snow seemed soft
and shallow and they fell asleep

beside the berry bushes
not far from where the bare grass
was brown and wet

and the trees were not
topheavy with snow.
At daybreak

Foster found the guides
lying beneath a tree
and he returned

for Eddy's gun.
The first shot
shook the others awake.

When they were on their feet
the survivors found
the guides dead

in the mud below
the tree and took advantage
of the opportunity

to make a meal
of the two men
though they were almost all bone

and they went on
singing in the winter woods
the childhood songs

that everyone knew,
and they held hands
each one a link

in a living chain
as they emerged from the trees
and limped into the light

where they sank
upon the grass. They were seen
the same day

by a band of diggers
who brought them around
behind a hill

where their village
stood hidden from the valley.
They gave them gruel

in a bowl
feeding them with their fingers
and pouring the broth between their teeth.

Later they ate
a handful
of acorn meal.

These were not
savages who dwell
in a cave

in a canyon wall;
they live hunched
over a pit

in a hut like this
one of ours . . .
When the whites

were well enough to walk
they were helped out of the huts
and removed

to the ranch
of a white couple
where they could recover

and this was where
Eddy had been found
by Moultry and his men
on their way to save us all.

26

My Friend Has Not Forgotten

Some could not be saved.
Moultry told me he would take
Wolfinger's widow
and Noah

and two
of Elizabeth's boys
who had fed

on their father
so they had
strength to walk.

They set out
hiking in heavy snow.
The rest of us

had to hope
for fair weather
to see them

safely over
the mountains
while we

were to wait
here in the hut
for Reed to arrive.

I never knew
what happened to these people
until the week

when James Reed
came into camp.
I was asleep

but Tamsen
whispered in my ear
and I awoke.

"Your friend is here,"
she said.
I was overjoyed.

"Show him in!"
I leaned
on one elbow;

I was unable
to lift
my right arm

for the pain,
and it hung down
on my hip.

Reed sat there
on the floor—
the first time

I had seen
his face
for five months.

Margaret was well
he said and all
his children were alive.

He had met
the party that went out
with Moultry—

"They will
reach the valley
if the weather will hold."

I wept.
He wiped my beard
with his handkerchief.

Here we were
together
as we were

last winter
laying plans to take
the trail

on trust,
when we were still bemused
by the myths of maps

and we were careful to equip
our company with an abundance of belongings
and all our hope

for the future.
But that was before
we came

to feel
the slow intelligence of the snow
groping over the ground

learning the shape
of the land and leaving it
in solitude

which seems
unnatural
to you and me

in its simplicty . . .
Of this we never spoke.
I merely thought

how good it is to know
my friend has not forgotten
those of us

who are hurt
too bad to travel
with their children

or like Tamsen
are reluctant to leave
the ones they love.

Unable to speak
I tried to stand.
I shut my eyes.

The pain flew from my hand
to the nape of my neck.
I seemed to swim around the room

and fell back
among the mud and old needles
and rolled to one side.

We were silent.
As soon as I could see that he was ready
I said it was all right

for him to go.
I said I understood the necessity
to start early

in the afternoon,
but when he ducked out of the door
I asked myself

what is death
that it should be a question
of this person

or that one
blessed with good
fortune

or lost
by bad luck.
I thought perhaps

it's better to know
you will die
in this place

than to suffer
ignorance of the event
and go on trying to guess

where it will be.
However, I was sorry
to think this

and when she was brought
to our hut
I said

"Goodbye—"
to the widow
of my brother

and sat up
on my bed
to give her

a kiss
so we could part
in peace.

"Ba'tiste will bring you
our children
one day soon,"

I told her
and she was led
away without a word.

Then they assembled
beside the creek
which was no more

than a noise
underneath the snow
and Reed assumed

the whole weight
of the woman—
Elizabeth

all but hung
upon his back.
Her boys could walk

though their feet
were frostbit
and they followed

their mother
toward the lake
where they would join

with others
to make the journey
to the valley.

When they had gone
the indians who live
in this territory

were overcome
by curiosity
and crept in

close to camp.
They chose to stop
as they reached the creek

where the trunk
and skull
of Jacob

lay in the snow
starting to thaw.
Tamsen sat

outside the hole
and tried to wave
for help.

She cried out
and they looked up
at our hut.

A dozen
of the young diggers
standing around

among the alders
wearing a simple square
of bear skin

or fox fur
or bobcat
or bare-ass altogether.

When they saw
we were still alive
they began to talk

to themselves.
Then they gave
up and left.

She did not come
back at once
but crawled out

onto the snow
and called
for Ba'tiste.

No answer.
She called his name
again. No one came.

She disappeared
from view
only to return

on all fours
creeping into the room
careful not to wake

our daughters
asleep in the arms
of each other.

She shook her hair
from her face
and said,

"I fear
that we're lost.
I went

to look for Ba'tiste
in his tent
but it's empty—

he has fled
and left us
to ourselves.

Our darlings
will die here.
What can we do?"

However,
we were soon
to learn

of more men
who had reason
to remain.

Even now
as we sat back
and saw the sun

shiver
over the snow
we were struck

with wonder
at the rich
enduring sound
of human speech.

27

After This Life
We Will Listen

When the relief party left
two grown men
Cady and Stone
were willing to stay behind.

We wondered why
until we could see
they were keeping watch

on our wagon
partly buried, by the creek, where the wheels
have warped

in the old snow
and the wet wagonbed
is bowed out at one end.

"When we're dead,"
I told Tamsen,
"they'll feel free

to unload it
and walk off with whatever
they find."

She said that
with a little luck they could uncover
even the money we had

to hide from Keseberg and his friends
late last spring
on the plains.

While we talked of what would happen
a queer thought crossed my mind.
"Why not pull

the quilt out
and cut it open?
Offer them all of our money

to take the children
now while they might
reach the valley alive."

It was worth a try
if the men agreed.
She wondered,

"Can we guarantee
their honesty?
What if they run away?"

I shared her worry
but I handed her my knife
and she walked at once to the wagon

to cut the quilt
and crossed back
with the money making a mound

beneath her bosom . . .
Meanwhile the men remained motionless
as their eyes

trailed her out of the trees
toward home not turning
her head now knowing

she could go nowhere
unseen and so she would let them look
and discover

what it was.
When she reached the hut
we called Cady and Stone to come over

and listen to our plan.
Stone walked across
the cold gloom

to the door where
he could see the money lying on the mud
inside the room.

While we conferred
huddled in the hole
once again it began to snow

and it was necessary
for them to hurry
and try to make the lake camp the same day

to have a roof overhead
on the first night they were away.
I said, "Their safety will depend on you."

"They have the same chance as Cady and me,"
he replied and ran off
to join his friend.

I told Tamsen, "You must go
when the girls do
and have no fear

for my peace of mind.
You can see
how it's going to be

if you stay here:
we'll both freeze
or else starve

in a few days
and what kind
of devotion does this show?

To lose your life because
you're my wife.
We both know

a man marries
a woman to bring to bed
and to be happy in the house

of his heart where they live
like an unquiet candle that will rise and fall
whichever way the wind draws

the licking flame
so it must consume itself night after night
until it dies and darkness fills the room.

Though there are no laws
to tell us in what manner
a mule marries

or our horses or sheep,
are we so different from the dumb
animals

that we must lie down
side by side to die in the same place?
Is life so cheap?

In the face of a fierce necessity
if it means no more
to you or me

than this loyalty
what good is marriage?
It's a blessing, and a true bargain,

but it's absurd
to keep me company
so we can die together in our sleep."

"I have worse worries
that need my attention,"
she said and sent the men to the wagon

to collect the wool clothes still in storage
among the remaining supplies.
She would stay regardless

so we turned to other matters
though we exchanged glances
as we dressed our daughters,

slender Eliza
and Georgia
and the infant Frances.

All their winter clothes but the boots
were a size too large or more.
Three huge hoods hid their eyes.

Their woolen mufflers wound
twice around their throats
and swung below their knees.

The sleeves hung down so far
that their hands didn't show.
Even when they were about to go

and were led out onto the snow
the girls still looked as if
they were clowning in their stiff coats.

Tamsen told how the men would leave them
with people we could trust
to treat them tenderly

and see that they were well fed
when it was possible.
Finally she said,

"For the sake of your father
and mother
wherever you live

whether you're with Elizabeth
or anyone else
be kind to one another

and always remember
to tell people
that your name is Donner."

We kissed them goodbye.
Cady and Stone caught up
the girls in their arms and went on their way.

When they were gone my wife walked out
upon the snow. I could see her breath
for a minute more beneath the branches

before she turned away. Then the back
of her cloth coat was all I could see
while she stood by the creek and cried.

A curtain of quiet snow drifted down
behind her, heavy enough to hide
her footprints in the frozen pack

as though this weather was a soft reproach
falling all winter in the sifting trees
while the ground grew indifferent to our touch.

She left the creek and hurried home to the mouth
of the hut and slipped inside
and sat on her bed

of old branches
to stay until the hour
of our death.

It wasn't my idea.
I told her to go.
We began to argue . . .

"How do you know it's too late?
You might make it if you try."
She never moved a muscle.

You can't say no
to Tamsen
or tell her what to do,

she won't hear you
talking whenever
she doesn't want to.

So we sit
and wait
and with warmer weather

the snow thaws
until a green patch
of the meadow may be seen

close to the creek.
Even in the hut we can hear
the persistent plink as the water drips

on the floor in a muddy pool.
We stay put
or sit up and watch

the birds perform outside the door,
and while we do
we are never alone.

Every day after dawn
the grey coyotes crawl
on their bellies underneath the bushes

and walk out and squat
a hundred feet from our hut—
ears in the air

and their eyes down
as they sniff at the patches of hair,
rolling the pine cones with their paws

while they browse beneath the trees
and trickle urine
on the blond bones.

With a full beard
flowing over the snowy breast
of his silk shirt

a man looking more like
a ghost goes by us
on his way

to see the dead
carcasses which he collects in the shelter
of the low shrubs.

Keseberg
hobbles past the huts;
his wide hat almost hides his face

as he reaches the mound
and crouches over the corpses
turning them this way and that

with one end of his staff,
a walking stick cut like a crutch,
a long piece of pine which he can cramp

under his arm.
He plants it in the moist mulch
to one side when he bends

over the bodies
and deliberately extends
his stiff leg inches off the ground.

He puts his waterbucket nearby.
He picks a skull from the pile beneath his knee
and plucks the brains and tucks them carefully

in his lap while he breaks
a breast apart and hunts with one hand
for the heart.

He takes up his stick when he wishes to go.
He carries the meat in the crook of his sleeve
and we watch him retreat

toward the trees
that protected my brother's place,
walking with a halting hitch in his hip

lifting his large leg
like a dead weight which he has had to drag
with him wherever he went.

A fire glows outside Jacob's tent.
When his dinner is done he tips
his bucket over the coals and we watch

as he moves down the meadow toward the woods
and disappears before dusk has come
quietly up to the door.

This silence
is soon broken.
The last days are like the first

mild morning
which arrives in April
when almost any noise is a surprise.

Squirrels race around the roof
scratching the thatchwork boughs.
They tumble down the dark walls

and leave us and leap onto the trees
where the birds shriek and sing.
Then one morning we hear

the alders rustle in the incessant rain.
Later the sun slips over the meadow
and the blue jays dive

in long dips
flashing from shadow to shadow,
while an enormous chorus fills the air.

After this life we will listen
lying in the loose grains of dirt
with our eyes sealed shut against the roots

that reach for them, we will hear
our breath begin again, the engine of the brain
begin humming in the mulch, and we will climb

with our nails, and teeth, biting through the damp earth
clawing away the soil, hand and mouth
tearing out of our wet tombs forever to find

it is Spring! The grass
is wet and waving toward the trees.
Their bark is yellow or brown and the leaves

are black on the underside that is so gentle
that we are afraid
to touch it.

Come into a meadow where the crystal snow-
crust shrinks under
the shade of the rocks . . .

After this life we will listen
to the judgments of bears and the deer
awaking.

The birds over the treetops, crossing and calling
in the long leaves.
The red eyes of berries

surprise us, and the deer
and the fox who know that we are there
on the brink of the meadow—

they can smell our fear,
floating into the grass like a shallow river
establishing its edges.

They find us and follow the cool water
from the mountains, their eyes bring the blue light
of evening onto the valley,

the prairie almost lost, drowning in darkness,
the sparks of stars already spinning
downstream, travelling in the tall weeds.

After this life we will listen
to the long river running thru the soil
saying it is Spring—

the sun has begun to burn
the brown needles nesting on the ground
around our graves.

The jays perch in the pines and cry
and wherever we may sleep
among the dead we will rise

together under the trees
like men who are set free
from the folly of a dream

into the fragrant morning
to hear the heavy stream
of our blood begin to sing,

our souls awake and warm once more
and weaving like a fire
when the light begins to dance
in the land of our desire.